P9-CMY-502

BE YOUR OWN
Dream
INTERPRETER

BE YOUR OWN
Dream
INTERPRETER

Uncover the real meaning of your dreams
and how you can learn from them

TONY CRISP

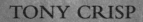

CICO BOOKS
LONDON · NEW YORK

For Jacqueline
In thanks for transformation

This edition published in 2018 by CICO Books
an imprint of Ryland Peters & Small Ltd
20–21 Jockey's Fields   341 E 116th St
London WC1R 4BW   New York, NY 10029

www.rylandpeters.com

First published in 2004 and 2008 as *Your Dream Interpreter*

10 9 8 7 6 5 4 3 2 1

Text © Tony Crisp 2004, 2008, 2018
Design and illustration © CICO Books 2004, 2008, 2018

A CIP catalog record for this book is available from the
Library of Congress and the British Library.

ISBN: 978-1-78249-656-4

Printed in China

Editors: Liz Dean and Mary Lambert
Design concept: Ian Midson
Illustrator: Jacqui Mair

Commissioning editor: Kristine Pidkameny
Senior editor: Carmel Edmonds
Junior designer: Eliana Holder
Art director: Sally Powell
Production controller: David Hearn
Publishing manager: Penny Craig
Publisher: Cindy Richards

CONTENTS

INTRODUCTION

Dreams have fascinated men and women throughout the ages. Through a great amount of experimentation into the nature and meaning of dreams and sleep, a vast amount has been learned, showing that dreams are more profoundly revealing of transforming insights and self-awareness than even ancient cultures realized. This flood of new understanding has shown that dreams are not mysterious jumbles of random images but arise from the innate mental and physical processes of life within us. This research has also defined techniques that each of us can use to understand the dramatic and graphic language of our dreams.

WHAT ARE DREAMS?

As with any area of thought, there are a wide variety of opinions as to what dreams are and what function they play in life. However, a synthesis of these views is that dreams are an expression of the most fundamental processes of life in us reaching toward awareness. Creatures have always dreamed, and in dreaming we see the biological life of our planet arriving at its own kind of consciousness, achieving it in a very different way than we know in our waking life. It is like a huge pool of collective awareness that is the experience of all living creatures. The psychiatrist Carl Jung called this shared awareness the Collective Unconscious. The Aborigines called it The Dreamtime. They recognized that all creatures emerge from it and pass back into it in sleep and dreams.

THE AMAZING EXPERIENCE OF DREAMING

Research into dreaming has shown that each of us dreams about four or five times each night. While we dream, our voluntary muscles no longer respond to our attempts to move, and our eyes move rapidly under closed eyelids. Our muscles are paralyzed in this way because if they were not, we would actually run around or act out what we are dreaming. Animals in which the brain area that blocks such impulses has been damaged do live out their dream in movement, practicing hunting or survival tactics. So we see that dreaming extends your range of experience to the point where you double or treble your experiential life span; while dreaming, it is as if you are living what is being dreamt.

WHAT WE CAN LEARN

This ability of the mind to play with experience or information, to rearrange it and try it in different guises, as one does in dreaming, is fundamental to the creativity and functioning of human life. Dreams reveal to you what you fail to see about yourself while awake. They show the directions you are taking in life and unveil things that lie beyond the boundaries of your five senses. But their information is sometimes obscured in apparently strange drama or feelings. Using the techniques presented within the following pages will enable you to gain insights that can transform the way you live, allowing you to release old tensions and hurts.

Part 1
INTERPRETING
YOUR DREAMS

Dream symbols are the language that our inner self uses to talk to us. In this section you will learn how to recall your dreams and interpret the themes and symbols that appear in them.

RECORDING YOUR DREAMS

Dreams express the unconscious wisdom that enables and sustains the growth and health of your body and mind. Every night, most of us have at least two sessions of sleep that produce several dreams, each of them unique. When you remember and record your dreams in detail, you consciously access your innate creativity. You become the creator and producer of your own drama, just as many artists, musicians, and writers have used their dreams as inspiration for their work.

Each dream provides its own message, and it is only by making a record that you will become aware of these messages. This book will help you record, examine, and interpret your dreams. Dreams often melt away as you wake, so write or recite your dreams every morning (see opposite) using a notebook or voice recorder. Record everything you remember. In addition to recording the details of your dreams, it is essential that you consider how the themes in your dreams relate to your daily life. Interpret the key images using the Directory (see pages 26–159). Recurring dreams (see page 22) are often sent to heal a major life issue; reliable dream recall can be the key to revealing what these issues are and how to confront them.

Ross Campbell and Robert Hoffman at Carleton University, Ottawa, Canada, carried out a research project on dream recall. They used three groups of students: Group One simply made a note of any dream remembered; Group Two wrote down the dream in as much detail as possible; and Group Three wrote the dream in detail, but in addition they also kept a personal journal of daily events. In other words, they reviewed and considered their day. Group Three remembered more dreams than Groups One or Two.

As you get used to recording your dreams, you will notice how rewarding the results are. Your recall will improve the more you practice so that no matter how random the images may seem, you will soon note the recurring characters, themes, and objects in your dreams; these make up the key symbols your unconscious is using to carry the vital messages to you.

TRY THIS **DREAM RECALL**

You may be one of those lucky people who easily remembers their dreams almost every morning. If you feel that you never dream or barely remember your dreams, work through the recall exercise below every day for about a month and you will be rewarded with a series of images and stories.

1. Place a notebook or journal by your bed. Before you fall asleep, try to spend a few moments imagining yourself waking up, remembering a dream, and then writing it down.

2. As you wake, move as little as possible. The process of forgetting our dreams as we wake each morning is stimulated by physical movement, so try to stay still for a few moments.

3. Gently hold in mind the question of what you dreamed. Imagine sinking back into the dimness of sleep, feeling your way back to your dreams. Your question is a fishing line that you drop into your unconscious. If you are quiet, a dream will take the hook.

4. Once you have remembered some images, and perhaps some fragments of the narrative, try to piece together the whole dream

story. Record it, with the date, in your journal. Write as full a description as possible. Give each dream entry a name.

5. Later in the day, read through your dream again. Do not attempt to interpret it at this stage. Simply consider whether the theme, characters, or images remind you of a previous dream. Make a note of any common elements in your journal or notebook.

6. If you are still not remembering many dreams, set your alarm clock to wake you about 45 minutes earlier than your usual time. Mentally associate the sound of the alarm with the question, "What am I dreaming?"

WHERE DO DREAMS COME FROM?

Science has revealed that all mammals dream and babies dream in the womb, so we know that humans were dreaming long before they could speak. We can therefore be certain that dreams arise from what lies beneath language and our thinking selves. They arise from feelings, from instinctive or passionate responses to events. Dreams flow from the formless energies and dynamics of life's processes. Images communicate these energies and processes to our waking selves. In most cases, they reach the level of myths, symbols, and dramatic expression. We respond to this, otherwise we would not be moved by theater, movies, or dance. Recognizing this process in your dreams is the first step to discovering a rewarding interpretation.

Now that you have written down your dream, examine it using the following questions:

WHAT IS THE PRIMARY ACTION OF MY DREAM?

What are you doing in your dream? Are you running away, showing affection, climbing a hill or a tree? You may experience one or more themes: solving a problem, searching for something, or going somewhere new.

For the moment, isolate your primary action from the context of that action in the dream. For instance, if you were climbing a hill, simply record it as "climbing." If you were searching a house, write it as "searching." Write these down in your journal as an annotation to the dream, and ask yourself how they apply to your waking life. For example, if you were searching in the dream, ask yourself if you are aware of searching for something in waking life, and if so, what? Take a few minutes to consider, and leave it to work in the back of your mind. If you gain an insight, write it in your journal.

Possible themes include: being trapped, starting something, building or renovating, relationships, being with others, being alone, leaving things behind, death, birth, and growth.

WHAT AM I FEELING IN THE DREAM?

Your feelings are often the main element of a dream, around which everything else is developed. Strip away the images and action of the dream and see if you can recognize what feelings are involved. If possible, feel something of what was felt in the dream and ask yourself what that feeling connects with in your waking life, when you first felt like that, and if that feeling occurred recently. In your journal, write down the feelings and any connections you make.

AM I ACTIVE OR PASSIVE?

This is a vital question, because your relationship with others in your dream may indicate your habitual response while awake. If you are the driving force in your dream, for example, this often reflects your active behavior in daily life. Passivity may be shown by:

* Not being the main character in your dream
* Others taking what is yours or blocking you
* People dominating you

Note signs of passivity and add this to your remarks about the dream in your journal. You can learn to transform passivity in your dreams by using visualization techniques (see page 17).

AM I AFRAID OF ANYTHING?

Some dreams reveal an anxiety, or something about yourself that you are avoiding. Fear is a natural and necessary part of life. It helps you avoid, or deal with, dangers. But in dreams it has a different role. Fear of your own feelings or urges can hinder your potential and isolate you from the full range of your abilities and feeling responses. For example, fear may lead you to turn away from an opportunity or a relationship that would have satisfied you. Such turning away means you are not experiencing your potential.

When a fear appears in a dream, even in the format of a nightmare, it usually means that you are ready to meet it. In your journal, note what the fear is, and through what theme or situation it is depicted. Read through the sections on dealing with nightmares (see pages 20–21) and controlling recurring dreams (see pages 22–23), for more detailed information on how to deal with fear more fully.

WHAT IS THE DRAMA OF MY DREAM?

The questions that you have looked at so far have clarified some aspects of your dream's meaning. Now you need to bring what you know into an overview of the dream. To do this, think of your dream not as something connected with you personally, but as a piece of drama that you might see on television. What is it saying to you? To some extent, this will have been defined through asking yourself what themes your dream contains, and what feelings were felt. But now you need to integrate these separate pieces of information. Bring them together in an overall view, and write them out as if you were describing to somebody else what your dream reveals about you and how it connects with your everyday life.

TO IMAGINE IS TO CREATE

Being able to visualize and work with your dream imagery and feelings has enormous benefits. Visualizing can enable you to gain greater insights into your dreams than you can experience by using the questions alone (see page 17). This is because many dreams leave questions unanswered. For example, fear dreams may not lead to a resolution of anxiety. Visualization allows you to work with, and transform, this situation. Visualization also enables you to have a fuller connection and involvement with your dream. You can enter into any character or environment your dream presents, then—almost magically—you can explore its qualities, weaknesses, and strengths, and see how these may add to, or detract from, your waking life.

YOU CAN ALTER YOUR DREAM TO FIND SATISFACTION

Remember that although there are no bad parts in dreams, a dream often leaves you feeling unsatisfied, incomplete, or even scared. This was Eve's experience.

Eve dreamed that she was in a small community. It was evening, and people had shut themselves in their homes because there was a strange dog loose on the streets. The dog wasn't "normal." It was ferocious, and if it got near you it would eat you. So Eve was looking for somewhere to hide, but she had no home.

After she woke up, Eve visualized herself back in the dream, facing the crazy dog. No matter what she did, the dog was still chasing her. Once she realized that the dog was the most important part of the dream, she imagined herself becoming the dog to see what it felt like. She

immediately sensed its anger and frustration. As she allowed herself to feel this, she understood that the dog was both afraid of, and angry with, people. Eve then recognized these feelings as her own. As a child, she had often been made to feel unwanted and rejected because she was of mixed racial parentage. As an adult, Eve was still cautious about allowing people into her life. She still felt some anger about how people had treated her. As this became clear, Eve understood her dream. She had been trying to hide from her own anger. People were shutting themselves indoors, suggesting that others sensed her hidden anger and were cautious. Eve then imagined knocking on doors apologizing, saying that the dog was hers, that it had been hurt as a puppy, and that she was now loving it.

Eve reentered her dream while awake, and explored it by playing with its imagery and noticing what she felt. She then used these insights to direct the dream to a satisfying conclusion. In this way, she changed the fear that led her to run away from the dog into a feeling of caring and social connection. But she also did something else in this imagined scene: She embraced the idea that she could alter her behavior in daily life. She did this by becoming consciously aware of the feelings created in the dream, and by experimenting with a new approach to people and to herself.

A great deal of research has been conducted on the effects of visualization. When used to improve performance, in sports, business, or relationships, visualization has been found to be 75 percent as effective as physical practice. Using visualization to explore your dreams helps you arrive at the sorts of insights and change that Eve discovered. It builds new blocks of experience and understanding that transform the way you respond to everyday events. It allows you to experiment, speeding up your personal growth.

When learning to visualize, it is helpful to be in a quiet, undemanding environment. As you gain mastery over the skill, you can use it in almost any situation.

1. Choose a "practice" dream that has fairly clear images, and is not too long or complicated. Sit quietly and allow any unnecessary tension in your body to melt away. Slow your breathing slightly, and think of your body as a television screen that you are going to watch. Now remember your dream, and imagine walking into it, moving into your dreamscape. You do not need to have very clear images of this, just the sense, however vague, of what is in the dream. What does it feel like? Watch the screen of your body to see if there are any slight shifts in feelings, or if certain memories or ideas suddenly come to mind.

2. When you have done this for a satisfying time, imagine that you are now one of the characters, animals, or objects in your dream. Try to see what it feels like to be them. It doesn't matter if they are somebody you know, such as a member of your family, or they are an animal, or even

a tree. Take time to explore how you feel, and notice if any memories or ideas arise.

3. To end the exercise, move from one of the people or objects to another reasonably quickly to see if you can sense any difference in the way you feel. This is important, because sometimes you will not become aware of what you are feeling until you shift perspectives.

SLEEPING ON A PROBLEM

A young woman, a computer programmer, recently told me that she had confronted a problem in her work. She had tried various approaches, but they had not succeeded. Yet the next morning, she awoke from a dream that had shown in detail what could be done to solve the problem. She tried it, and it worked.

Creativity and the ability to solve problems are not restricted to geniuses. We all have the potential to develop and harness the creative impulse. Unfortunately, many of us have had our creative abilities suppressed. We are often told to avoid failure rather than use it as a step toward problem-solving. Trained in the acute recognition of our limitations, we can become blind to the unbounded possibilities of the mind and creativity.

CREATIVE DREAMING

Dr. Frank Barron, a research psychologist at the University of California Institute of Personality Assessment, compared 5,000 creative individuals with others in their field with a similar intelligence quotient (IQ). The data showed that creativity and problem-solving do not depend upon having a high IQ.

Other research in problem-solving and creativity shows that the human mind has possibilities that are rarely used. When dreaming, many of the limitations that we place upon ourselves through our learned attitudes fall away. In the

dream state, we have access to our total memory. The subliminal perceptions we gather every day through body language, relationships, and the many things we take in out of the "corner of our eye" are accessible, so our creativity, problem-solving capability, and ability to arrive at insights are magnified.

TRY THIS SOLVING A SPECIFIC PROBLEM

When learning to visualize, it is helpful to be in a quiet, undemanding environment. As you gain mastery over the skill, you can use it in almost any situation.

1. What is your problem? Have you already explored all the ways you can think of to solve it? Dreams do not usually respond creatively to waking inertia. They are stimulated by your efforts to learn or wrestle with a real-life problem. So, define your question. This should be done with one single issue in mind, and not be several questions in one. So it might be a question like, "What should I guard against in this issue?", "Which direction should I take?", or "What sort of relationship can I expect from my new lover?" An example of how not to frame a question by asking several questions in one would be, "Will the relationship with my new boyfriend work, or if not, should I go back to my husband, or should I simply concentrate on my job?"

2. Write the question on a piece of paper and stick it somewhere you will see it often during the day. Then, when you go to bed, review the question and ask for a response from your dreams. On waking, record whatever you dreamed. Consider any possible links with your question and what the dream is commenting on.

Remember that dreams are showing you a possibility, and there are infinite perspectives on any situation. So, although the dream might be showing you the highest probability for resolving your problem, it is not an ultimate truth.

DEALING WITH NIGHTMARES

When explored, nightmares always show themselves as an attempt to heal a past hurt or a present fear. To understand this, it is helpful to form a picture of the two polarities of daily experience. One polarity is your waking state. In this state, you generally feel distinct and separate from others. You see yourself as an object moving about the world, and you know the vulnerabilities of your body and mind. Your particular experiences and thoughts color the way you feel about existence. Tragic events in your life may have left psychological scars. The other polarity is that of sleep. To fall asleep, your ego has to surrender all effort and will. As you enter sleep, you lose awareness of yourself as a separate individual. Experiments that have allowed people to enter this realm of sleep with some awareness say that body awareness disappears. Your sense of self melts as if it were a drop of water merging into an ocean. This merging brings healing, and in dreams this wholeness attempts to flow through to our waking self.

However, the fears and tensions that we have gathered act as blocks. These blocks are pushed to the surface by the action of dreams when our ego is strong enough for them. This is what we experience as a "nightmare." The block, or traumatic experience, is like a frozen chunk of emotion, or an attitude stuck in one position, which stops you from flowing freely with the changing current of life. You may have been hurt in love, or had your trust betrayed, and so some of your feelings and attitudes are held tight. Allowing them to become conscious and learning to understand their cause means they can melt away.

Some nightmares are about present fear. These nightmares offer the same opportunity for healing. Such fears usually arise from an unbalanced view of who and what we are. When the waking and the sleeping self are balanced, the fear usually disappears.

TRY THIS **MEETING YOUR MONSTERS**

1. Remember that while you are dreaming, things are dramatized and felt very deeply. So do not fear that something will overwhelm you. Dreams and nightmares are a part of your self-balancing process.

2. Imagine yourself back in the dream and meeting the frightening thing or scary situation. Notice how you feel and what changes occur in your body. If you have this attitude of quiet watching, with the intent of understanding and helping the healing process, memories often arise. For instance, a man woke from a nightmare in which a terrifying creature was trying to get at him and a child. He then imagined himself allowing the creature to reach him. Next he remembered the fear he felt as a child from living in a war zone, and recognized that this fear had prevented him from leading a freer and less restricted life.

3. Visualize yourself developing a different relationship with the fearful thing or situation. Take time with this, as it needs to reach into areas of experience that you have probably kept buried.

4. If you find it difficult to visualize or enter the dream, draw or write down the dream and its characters. If you draw it, you can change it to deal with the central fear in a different way. This is helpful for children, too. The "creature" can be put in a cage, or in a less threatening situation. The aim is to play imaginatively with words or images until you feel at ease with the nightmare.

5. Have a dialogue with the fearful thing. Sometimes it helps to have two chairs—you can start the dialogue in one chair, then shift to the other chair to get a response. Ask it why it is appearing in your dreams in this scary way. What does it want from you? What can you do to change things? If you imagine yourself as the "thing" and say whatever arises, this can produce great insight.

UNDERSTANDING RECURRING DREAMS

Dreams do not usually occur unless there is something you haven't realized or dealt with. They indicate that something needs attention. Recurring dreams are sometimes like chores that haven't been done, and so they keep pushing into your awareness. In some dreams, the theme and action are almost identical. In others, the theme develops over time. The following dream is one that recurs for many people.

I have a disturbing recurring dream. There is a baby, so small it fits into my palm. I know it should be fed but I always forget. I leave it until the last moment to pick it up and give it a bottle. It looks at me with sad eyes as if to say, "Why do you do this to me?" —Lydia

Lydia's dream is about neglect. In some way, she is not nourishing a facet of her own personality. Because it is a baby in the dream, it probably depicts her need for love and support. Most recurring dreams are calling out for our attention. If we give such a dream just a bit of our time they will be transformed, either into a dream with a similar theme, or they will disappear altogether.

Recurring dreams deal with subjects that are as varied as the challenges and opportunities that we face. Try not to have a preconception of what your recurring dream may be saying. It can simply be about an attitude that is not allowing you to experience the sort of freedom you are capable of, or it may be a nudge asking you to be aware of something. We may know in the back of our mind that there is a danger we are not attending to—say, a loose floorboard—and recurring dreams are sometimes the voice urging us to take care or action.

TRY THIS DEALING WITH RECURRING DREAMS

1. A recurring dream is important, so take time with it. Work through the questions regarding the theme of the dream and your feelings (see pages 12–14). Write down and consider what you arrive at.

2. In a quiet situation, talk yourself through the dream again as if you were dreaming it. Do this by imagining yourself in the dream and going through the experiences. Speak out loud, describing the dream in the first person and using the present tense. As you do so, take note of any feelings or memories that arise, and allow yourself to feel or explore them.

3. Have a dialogue using the two-chair method with any characters in your dream (see Meeting Your Monsters, page 21). Alternatively, you can simply "talk" to the dream as a whole, asking it such things as, "What is your message? I am unclear and really am trying to understand." Then to get the response, try to take on the feeling and attitude of listening, and simply allow any spontaneous feelings and ideas to arise. Afterward, make a note of any insights you experience in your journal.

Part 2
THE DREAM DIRECTORY

Many common dream themes and symbols are included in this alphabetical directory to help you draw out the hidden meanings of your dreams, whether they are unique or recurring.

A

ABANDONMENT

Fear of abandonment is one of the most powerful of childhood feelings, so your dream may be representing this fear because certain events have made it resurface. Look at your everyday experiences to see if you can discover its source or cause. If you are abandoned and left alone, this could mean you are experiencing loneliness, neglect, or insecurity in relationships. Feelings of abandon or giving way to your emotions represent a lowering of your moral standards, finding new freedom, or releasing pent-up feelings. If your dream shows you abandoning someone else, this may express hidden anger, or mean that you are not nurturing some part of your personality. Sometimes, dreaming about abandonment may involve feeling dependent, or supporting dependents.

ABDOMEN

In general, the abdomen refers to your ability to respond in an emotional, sensual, and intuitive way. It also depicts your ability to digest or reject experience and food. So if you eat poisonous fruits or suffer sad emotions, there is pain. Your dream may be about your physical health or diet needs. If so, it will in some way be connected with food or activities that bring illness or health. If you are shot, stabbed, or punched in the abdomen, it usually indicates being emotionally hurt or physically injured. For example, losing a loved one may cause actual abdominal pain. Harsh criticism can also produce the same sort of hurt and dream.

ABNORMAL

Depending on whether the abnormal feature in your dream is part of your body, someone else's body, or of the dream objects or surroundings, it suggests two things:
1. You may be harboring fears about your self-image. Or the dream may reflect fears about your physical health. Even if these abnormalities appear on someone else, it may still refer to you, perhaps a part of you that has not developed to its full potential, or has been hurt.
2. If the abnormality is part of the dream environment, it may suggest you sense that something is not right, either with what is happening around you, or how you are responding to it.

ABOVE

The position suggests a wider view, superiority, or perhaps an advantage. If something or someone is above you in your dream, it can indicate that you feel disadvantaged, or lacking in power, or that you are in awe of something or someone. Perhaps you feel that something or somebody is beyond your reach.

ABROAD

Being abroad, or mention of a country other than your home, is in general a way of expressing your particular feelings or situation. For example, if Italy is abroad for you, you may see it as a warm and romantic place and this will be represented in your dream. But seeing a country at war represents conflict. So in most cases, being abroad suggests a change or a different feeling or life situation than your current one. The dream may refer to exploring new interests, or new areas of yourself, or even of being in an uncomfortable situation. If you have visited that country, the dream most likely refers to the events or emotions that occurred while you were there. If the country is a place your family originated from, it may depict the unconscious influences and cultural attitudes you inherited from them. If you have lived or worked in that country, you need to define whether you were happy or stressed there, and what you absorbed of the atmosphere, because the dream is referring to this.

ABUSE

Being abused, or abusing, physically or sexually, may point to your own past

experiences. The dream may be an attempt to work out feelings you have about these events. Of course, we often abuse our own body and mind by the things we do, such as drinking alcohol and eating junk food, so the dream may be indicating this.

ABYSS

Seeing an abyss usually represents the unknown, or perhaps the depth of your own mind or consciousness. The fear of falling into the abyss represents your attempt to control your feelings and what is inside yourself. It can refer to feelings about, or fear of, death. Seen in a positive light, it links your conscious mind with the immense potential you hold within. Part of this potential is an experience of going beyond opposites, of resolving paradoxes, of moving beyond the limitations of the rational mind and emotional responses. In these ways it is similar to dream images of the sea. (*see* Sea)

ACCIDENT

In your dreams there are no accidents or chance events—you create the whole dream, so to dream of an accident may mean you sense that attitudes or events are leading you toward whatever the dream depicts. This is not a prophecy, but it may occasionally depict a self-fulfilling incident, so be aware of any events suggesting what is portrayed in your dream. This enables you to avoid the final moves creating the accident. The dream may also show stress or tension that can lead to events best avoided. The event may be a breakup, work crisis, or whatever the dream suggests. Sometimes this shows the feelings it gives rise to, such as shock or fear. Perhaps something has upset or hurt you. An accident in a dream can indicate feeling out of control or extremely stressed.

ACCUSATION

This indicates feelings of guilt, or social or relationship difficulty. If you are the accuser, it may show feelings of being victimized or wronged, possibly in the distant past.

ACHE

An ache is a warning that all is not well. Some part of your body is damaged, or your dream could be using your body symbolically. A heartache may suggest emotional hurt, or a problem with your legs can represent a lack of confidence. (*see* Arms, Head, Illness, Legs)

ACORN

With its power of growth, the acorn, or any seed in a dream, can depict a hidden but wonderful potential. It can also represent change, starting something new, or growing stronger.

ACTING

If you are the actor/actress in your dream, you may be playing a role. This dream may also express a desire for public acclaim or notice. But if you have strong feelings or ideas about the person's character, your dream image may be using them to represent those feelings or ideas. Just as someone's life may be "acted out" on stage or in a film, so actors may represent different parts of your own life. (*see* Roles, Stage)

ADDICTION

Something or someone may be influencing you in a way that undermines your ability to make choices. There may also be a connection with powerful emotional or economic dependence. These activities or influences are not arising from your will or responsibility, but from the emotions and fears that are symbolized by the addiction in your dream. You can be addicted to a relationship, or to work, and your dream may be commenting on that situation. If so, it is wise to consider moving toward greater independence. If someone else is addicted, the other person may represent a part of your character.

ADDRESS

Your home address is your condition or status in life, or your life situation. If it is another person's address, it suggests you identify with that person. You will need to look for clues as to what your dream is telling you about this. It may indicate contact. A past address means you are dealing with things you learned or felt while you lived at the previous place—a past way of life, perhaps. A new address can signify changes you are making in some way, and forgetting your address shows confused feelings about what your life situation is. Ask yourself if you have lost sight of your goals or standards. (*see* House)

ADMIRATION

If you are admiring someone else, this may be directing you to become aware of qualities that you either need to develop, or need to recognize. Being admired suggests you either need some appreciation, or you are noticing qualities in yourself. If the dream stresses that you are greatly admired, it may suggest that you have an inflated opinion of yourself, or perhaps you have a strong need for approval and special acclaim from others.

ADULTERY

Everyone has sexual desires about people other than their partner. Sometimes they relate to people with whom it can be difficult to have a sexual relationship. If you are having sex with another person, the dream may refer to sexual release. This is a harmless way of exploring sex with another person. If you dream your partner is having sex with someone else, you may be feeling uncertain of your own value and wondering whether you are lovable. These feelings may hide painful dependence on your loved one. Making love to someone you dislike can

mean you are getting involved with distasteful things.

ADVENTURE

The dream is probably a comment on changes you are making within yourself, or in your external life, or perhaps both. It shows you taking risks, exploring something new. The context in the dream will state whether the risk is worth taking, or whether fears or other factors hold you back.

ADVICE

Whether the advice is given or received, this often suggests information you need to think about, and perhaps act upon.

AFFAIR *see* Adultery

AFRAID *see* Fear

AGE/AGELESS/AGING

The age of characters, family, animals, or objects or your own age in a dream often carries very definite associations or information. What these associations are depends a great deal on your age. If the person is ageless, it depicts the part of you, your fundamental core, which does not change. A baby or child refers to your feelings of dependence or vulnerability, perhaps even helplessness or powerlessness. But often it suggests a need for love, support, and care; it may even represent memories of being a baby or childhood. Extreme old age suggests feelings about death, an old way of life, or an influence in yourself or surroundings that pre-dates your birth. Influences from family, such as attitudes or fears, may be generations old, so they may be depicted as incredibly ancient. This in turn represents something with a lot of wisdom or experience. You may therefore feel the person is holy or revered in such dreams.

A middle-aged person represents achievement, maturity, or the aging process. An older person may depict feelings about your parents or a parent/authority figure, the wisdom gathered from many years of living; your declining power or creativity; or feelings about aging, decline, and loss within you. So an older person in your dream may refer to feelings you have about a parent or grandparent, such as dependency, love, or anger. A teenager can represent whatever difficulties you faced, or are facing, in the process of meeting sexual drives, adult relationships, and the need to become a motivated part of society. So there may be uncertain feelings, shyness, inexperience, or idealism suggested in the dream teenager (*see* Teenager). The young adult points to yourself at that age or period of life, at your physical peak—a period of worldly opportunity.

AGGRESSION

If you or someone else in your dream expresses anger or aggression, it still relates to your own feelings. It must be remembered that aggression or fear—fight or flight—is a fundamental response to threat. The more threatening your environment becomes or appears to be, the more fantasies or dreams of aggression you will experience. Alternatively, you may become passive and withdrawn or cower, which is another form of response to external stress, or fear of it. Therefore some aggressive dreams, whether practiced against someone else, or yourself, may have their origins in external threat or fear of it. Such dreams or fantasies may be a form of preparation to defend yourself or find an escape from the threat or an appropriate response to it. Hostility toward society or authority sometimes becomes directed inward and is self-destructive. This hostility can make you unable to express yourself, causing illness and a lack of self-belief. Meeting anger, aggression, and hostility in your dreams is healthy, and does not make you suppress it or express it socially. Therefore, consider what the anger is about, when it dates from, and in what way you can safely release it now. (*see* Anger)

AIR

Dreams use air in two ways. The first way depicts the sort of feelings you have if you have ever struggled to breathe through illness or danger. So the lack of air can show a struggle to survive in the present situation. Air also is often used as the medium through which you fly in dreams. In these dreams, the air probably

Babies and children

As birth and childhood are so formative in your development, most dreams that include a baby or child express some feelings that were formed in your early years. Children have wonderful potential, a great ability to learn, and vast curiosity. When we are children, we feel love and anger with great passion, and usually the first people this emotion flows to are our parents. These feelings can still dominate the way we deal with others as adults; we may still feel soul-crushing pain when the person we love leaves or betrays us. This arises from the child alive in us. We may want to possess,

or forever be desperately wanted by, our partner. We rarely see this constant love, yet our inner child takes no notice. So your dream child shows your emotions at an earlier age. Events may have stopped a particular line of growth—for example, you may have stopped loving a parent at a certain age because they deserted you. Out of this, your ability to love would have remained stuck at that age level.

Baby dreams can also link to pregnancy, new beginnings, and reclaiming joy and eagerness.

represents the invisible social atmosphere in which we unconsciously exist and strive. Therefore, occasionally a dream shows the dreamer losing the air or wind out of their sails that sustains their flight, suggesting a loss of support usually gained from public acceptance or approval, or even their own confidence.

AIRPLANE

Being in a plane indicates that you are making changes, or altering your situation in some way. It may also connect with a desire to get away from your present lifestyle, or suggest a business opportunity, or a desire for love.

In dreams where you watch an aircraft take off, or fly, it can point to a project you have launched, or an undertaking you are trying to "get off the ground." There are many analogies you can use in your dreams connected with a plane. For example, a crash landing may indicate problems ahead causing a difficult end to plans, projects, or hopes. Taking off shows the beginning, the launch, the rising excitement of what you are doing, or where you are going in life. Being attacked or bombed by aircraft can indicate anxiety attacks, or feeling threatened. A grounded plane represents difficulties in getting your plan, relationship, or hopes off the ground. Doing or seeing aerobatics or stunts suggests you are, or will be, daring in your life or undertakings, but often links to relationships, work, or personal growth. The success or failure of the flying will show how fearful or confident you are in expressing your daring. This is largely a matter of nerve, and feelings of anxiety can bring you down.

AIRPORT

This symbol concerns making changes, an urge to get somewhere other than where you are, or to achieve goals. It depicts the things that drive you to undertake journeys, to make changes, such as a need for love, a need to escape or leave things behind. Sometimes, it shows you reaching for independence, depending upon the details of the dream. So the airport can show a turning point in your life. Occasionally, it relates to the departure of a loved one or the end of a relationship.

AISLE

An aisle usually indicates a way you can move through obstacles or a lot of people. It suggests a method or attitude you are using to get to where you want. But it may also confront you with other people seeking their own ends, and put you in the limelight. In other words, your attempts to gain your own ends can make you stand out. (see Corridor)

ALCOHOL

Drinking can represent a transforming process. It portrays an influence that can change the way you act for better or worse. You need to consider your dream to see which of these it is. It can also represent stimulation, relaxation, and a way to face inner anxieties, even if only temporarily. Occasionally, it refers to a power you possess that can transform you. (see Drunk)

ALCOHOLISM see Addiction

ALIEN

This can be something you do not understand about yourself. It usually refers to a misunderstood part of you that is foreign to the rest of your character. If you feel isolated in the dream, it may suggest you feel alienated from others. Or it can link with your timeless side. This is because aliens have come to represent an influence from the stars, something from beyond what we understand. It can therefore depict the deep unconscious or spiritual core of oneself. (see UFO)

ALLERGY

This may show an allergy you have. Or it may be used symbolically. If so, consider what is represented by your allergy. Look it up in this directory.

ALLEY

This represents limited possibilities. An alley with a dead end suggests concern about a tight situation or direction that appears to have no way out. (*see* Highway)

ALLIGATOR

The alligator or crocodile is similar to the serpent and depicts the power of unconscious emotions and fears. If you do not relate to your unconscious urges constructively, conflict can occur. This can make you feel scared of these forces inside you, making you fearful of being swallowed, dragged down into dark feelings, or becoming irrational. (*see* Reptile)

ALPHABET

Seeing this symbol may refer to childhood, or to basic lessons in life.

AMBULANCE

Generally, an ambulance expresses your feelings that something is wrong, or shows an anxiety about health, or the health of someone close. Such dreams often depict life-threatening situations, and so deal with anxieties.

AMBUSH

This may signify an intuitive feeling about something being planned by others. But sometimes it is paranoia about being victimized. If you are creating the ambush, then you may be feeling angry about what someone is doing, or using underhand methods for your own ends.

AMPUTATION

This dream can be a symbol of losing the power that is represented by the limb depicted. (*see* Arms, Legs, Left, Right)

AMUSEMENT PARK *see* Fairground

ANCHOR

This indicates a part of your makeup that holds you firm to a task or code, such as determination, love, etc. But it has a deeper meaning; for the anchor reaches the seabed, or deepest part of your unconscious self. So it suggests a power of resolve or security coming from deep within. Or it may suggest being tied down. If the anchor is not holding, it shows influences that are weakening your confidence, or difficulties in meeting the influences affecting you.

ANCIENT

Something ancient can point to life experiences that are deeply buried, or even forgotten, such as childhood experiences, or to the person you were in a past relationship or job. It can also represent the deeply unconscious wisdom in your body, or in your racial memories or family traditions. Therefore, it can sometimes indicate inherited knowledge and your instincts that are older than your personality. But in general, it is knowledge or wisdom gained through long experience.

"Falling dreams" may be seen as fear of losing control, but they can also signify letting go of control. When you fall, you have to let go, and this can show that it is sometimes necessary to let old attitudes and perspectives fall away.

ANESTHETIC

This is an attitude or experience that is making you unconscious of what is happening. Something is deadening your feelings and sensitivity. Because anesthesia puts you to sleep, this dream image sometimes links with death, or an encounter with something that creates a wider awareness than offered by your senses.

ANGEL

The angel can represent the positive side of a relationship with someone you love, such as your mother or grandmother. It can also depict religious concepts, feelings, or intuitions about death, or a need for a parent figure to guide or instruct you in decision making. It can also represent innate wisdom. Angels are often associated with death or dying, or the communication of an important message.

ANGER/ANGRY

Like fear, anger is one of the fundamental and instinctive responses to a situation or pain, a danger, or an attack. It involves a lot of physical and emotional energy, and if blocked or repressed may cause psychosomatic illness or hurt. Therefore, it is important to acknowledge anger in your dreams, and find ways of expressing it without directing it at other people. Remember that an angry response is one of the ways you cover up hidden pain or upset. Accepting that it is okay to express your anger in your dreams encourages better physical and emotional health. (see Aggression)

ANIMAL

Dream animals are images of your most basic instinctive feelings and responses. The "fight or flight" response, for example, is part of our animal or inherited behavior. The underlying natural feelings we have about wanting a partner to love and with whom we could possibly have children are also expressions of the animal in us, as is the caring and love we can give to our children and each other. But our social training from infancy may have put us at odds with parts of our natural heritage. This is shown in our dreams when we run terrified from an animal or when we meet a wounded creature.

We also develop personal association from our relationships with our pets and the animals around us. Therefore, some animal dreams may display such diverse associations as a personal need for affection, a desire to be touched, or the need to care for another creature and feel needed. It can even be pregnancy and parental caring.

Sometimes in dreams you meet a shining animal, or one that is deeply loving or wise. It may speak to you and tell you things that on waking you realize are profoundly perceptive. This is because such a dream character is an image of your unconscious connection with your insight.

APARTMENT *see* House

APE

An ape can depict the physical, instinctive, wild, animal person that is within you. But it can also represent your inner wisdom. In this case, it refers to the instinctive knowledge of social relations, sex, and parenting. (*see* Animal)

APOCALYPSE *see* End of the World

APPOINTMENT

To dream of an appointment may mean that you need to remember something important about a relationship. Or it can suggest you unconsciously feel you are about to meet someone or something.

ARGUMENT

This can refer to a conflict or indecision. It may also indicate unexpressed feelings.

ARMOR

This represents the rigid emotional or intellectual barrier you may use to protect yourself from being hurt, frightened, or influenced by others.

ARMS

Arms represent your power to express emotions, desires and ideas, to construct or destroy. They may also be referring to your ability to love, give, take, create, defend, or reach out. Injury to an arm suggests loss of power to act or to support action, an inability to reach out or create. The left arm indicates your supportive feelings if you are right-handed; the right arm is your extroverted actions. (*see* Body, Left, Right)

ARRESTED/ARRESTING

This literally means to be stopped. If it is by a policeman, then you are probably restraining yourself morally with self-imposed rules or social restraints. You may feel some of your urges are "unlawful" or wrong. If you suffer anxiety dreams because of a previous fearful relationship with authority or police—for example, if you have survived a harsh political regime and are terrified of being arrested—then you need to seek help to heal the damage from these experiences.

ART/ARTIST

This is the display of an inner idea, feeling or direction, or the expression of inner thoughts that can be a source of self-realization. The artist may represent the urge toward fruition or self-realization. The art object, however, can depict some meaningful understanding within yourself that is not yet clear enough to put into words. (*see* Painting, Roles)

ASCENDING/ASCENT

There are several possibilities for this symbol in your dream. One is that passion, excitement, energy, or enthusiasm is rising. Getting higher is also often linked to your ability to see further, or your ability to become aware of a wider experience or a more inclusive viewpoint. It can involve change—leaving one place to arrive at another. So there may be the leaving behind of what was in the lower place. Occasionally, it involves ascent, especially if there is an irrational element in the dream, such as going out through the roof of a house in an elevator. This can suggest some excessive, possibly manic excitement. Lastly, we can climb up stairs, a tree, or to another high place, to escape any perceived danger or to deal with our fears. If this symbolism appears in your dream, ask yourself what you are trying to escape.

ASTHMA

This illness is associated with struggling to survive, or being smothered in a relationship, environment or situation, or it can represent anxiety. (*see* Air)

ASTRONAUT (*see* Space)

ATOMIC BOMB

This symbol often shows you that enormous changes are taking place within yourself, or are about to take place. This is because the old way of life can be destroyed or lost by some sudden change. But the bomb may also depict anxieties about your future, or the way of life surrounding you. Whichever feelings are most appropriate, the bomb usually shows enormous potential energy.

ATTACK

If you are being attacked, the dream usually arises because in some way you are repressing, in conflict with, or are frightened of your own emotions, sexuality, or anger. Occasionally, the fear is about your own potential or expanded awareness. If you are attacked by an animal, the repression or fear relates to your own natural primal urges. Sometimes, your dreams show an animal as depicting someone who you feel is expressing anger toward you. If you are attacked by a shadowy or frightening figure, it usually points to old childhood fears and hurts. If you are the attacker, this is more positive, as you are not being passive and hurt in your dreams. But you are still experiencing a conflict with whatever it is you are attacking. The object of your attack is probably a part of your own personality, so it may be better to meet it in some other way.

ATTIC

This may refer to your mind, or if the attic has things stored in it, then perhaps it indicates past memories or things you have not accessed for a while. Being trapped in an attic suggests that you are limiting yourself to a purely intellectual way of looking at life, or that you are caught up in the past. Alternatively, it may show that you are isolating yourself from ordinary life. (*see* House)

AUDIENCE

Standing in front of an audience may depict that you are trying to express something important, or deciding how you will "play out" your life or some situation. You may also be trying to get people's attention or be applauded for what you are doing. If you are in an audience, your unconscious may be showing you something important on the stage in front of you. This is because it may be difficult for you to become aware of it in any other way.

AUTUMN *see* Fall

AVALANCHE

Anything relating to snow can point to long-frozen emotions and urges. The avalanche may show that something is disturbing inner feelings that have lain cold and apparently dead for a long time.

AWAKE

This shows you "waking up" and becoming aware of something.

AXE

This represents material power or authority. It can indicate a desire to hurt or destroy, or it can be a fear of these emotions. (*see* Weapons)

B

BABY

This represents your infant self. Or some part of you that is still in the early stages of development and needs nurturing in case it dies. This is your inner potential. As such it may represent a new phase of your life, a new project, or a new way of life. Depending upon what is happening to the baby, it may also represent the infant part of you that needs love and help to release traumatic emotions. Or perhaps some aspects of infant feelings were not grown out of, such as an intense need for bonding. It can also show a great dependence on a partner's emotions.

BACK

In general, the back of someone or something usually refers to being unconscious, or to unknown things, things that are out of sight. If it is the back of a house it means being more private, less formal, or a hidden social situation. If this is your physical back, it is your strength or moral uprightness, or what is past.

BACKPACK

This often represents karma, the load of positive and negative attitudes, resentments and habits that you carry from your past, or which you have inherited. It is also the wisdom, insight, and talents you carry, perhaps unconsciously, or alternatively it can be anything that seems to be a burden.

BACTERIA *see* Germs

BAG

This represents female sexuality. But if it is a purse (handbag), it often stands for your sense of identity and ability to get your social needs fulfilled or identified. So it can show what you feel about yourself as a social force, or what you carry with you. You may be feeling a loss of self-esteem, for instance. A bag may hold something valuable and represent protection or the ability to hide something. (*see* Luggage)

BAKER

This is a power within you that can transform everyday life into something enjoyable. Because we use the word "dough" to suggest money, there can be a financial link. (*see* Roles)

BALANCE

This shows your ability to judge and discriminate, to measure one thing against another. It may also suggest a conscience that judges outer acts.

BALD *see* Hair

BALL
If it is a ball game, the ball may depict something about a relationship and what is going on. Or, it may represent competition and ways to win or play the game of life, love, or business. The ball can also stand for wholeness. (*see* Games)

BALLOON
This indicates light-hearted party feelings to do with celebration, or something insubstantial that can easily be destroyed or suddenly lost.

BAND (musical)
If it is a particular band or group, it may link with what you feel about them. Otherwise, it can depict feelings you have at the moment about working in harmony with others, or expressing your own creativity. Sometimes, this refers to teenage feelings and emerging sexuality.

BANDAGE
This represents feeling hurt, or a fear of injury. The bandage also connects with healing and sometimes death.

BANK
Linking with money, this symbol can connect with your feelings about it. So it can relate to security, worry, or getting or not getting the things you want. Money

and banks also associate with emotional and personal resources, the potential you have used or spent. (*see* Money)

BAR
What happens in the bar may indicate how you relate to social relationships. A public bar can represent a sense of pleasure, love of company and entertainment, or sometimes the place where you experience changes in yourself (shown by the influence of alcohol or spirits). It can also represent retreating—perhaps from home or a relationship. (*see* Alcohol)

BARBER *see* Hairdresser

BARRICADE
This represents the defense you use against others, or defensive events used against you. It may be an excuse, such as "I'm too ill to go to work," or "I'll never get anywhere, so what's the use of trying." (*see* Armor, Fence)

BASEMENT
This area represents hidden motives, unconscious, unknown feelings, memories or past experiences. It can also be your biological past, or the place where your conscious mind contacts hidden powers, universal wisdom, and even other minds. Sometimes, it can mean base deeds, low morals, or underlying dislikes. It is from the basement, below, or within, that libido, or life energy, arises. Fears and terrors

sometimes come from this space, because it is in the unconscious that we hide old memories and hurts. But it also contains the understanding of your essence. (*see* House)

BATH

The bathtub or bathing may remind you of feeling relaxed, of being more presentable and acceptable. It may also indicate healing and change. (*see* Water)

BATTERY

This is energy—your life force. If the battery is low or damaged, it may indicate health problems.

BATTLE

This is usually connected with conflict, the sort of battles you fight within yourself over love or anger, over feeling betrayed or being ignored. Another possibility is that of being attacked, or feeling attacked by others. You can also be fighting against the effect of fears, doubts, and memories. This can be especially true if you have been in a battle scene in waking life.

BEACH

This symbol indicates the borderline between your unconscious and conscious self. To find something on the beach is to find something that has come from deep within. It is the point of connection between your conscious self and all that exists in the background of your body and mind. (*see* Sea)

BEAR

This can represent a possessive mother, and the feelings this has aroused. But often, the bear indicates a meeting with dangerous emotions such as anger. There may be associations with independence or strength. (*see* Animal)

BEARD

This represents male feelings. It is also often used to show great wisdom, authority, or even saintliness, such as when the person has a white beard. If the beard is very long, it can symbolize great age, eternal life, or wisdom of the ages. Some people use a beard to hide their youth or bad skin, so it can be some sort of mask, or desire to be hidden. (*see* Hair)

BEAST

An animal of extraordinary power or a creature causing great terror is a feature of many dreams or nightmares. The figure may be partly human, or an animal that has strange characteristics. Or perhaps a figure that never quite declares itself, remaining unseen but causing or projecting great fear. In some dreams, the beast takes the form of a prehistoric creature. Overall, it represents our natural primal responses, from which we gradually mould our social and intellectual self. Unless we make friends with our beast, there may always be conflict between the rational and non-rational. (*see* Animal)

BED

There are many associations you may have with a bed. It can represent rest, sleep, unconsciousness, sexual pleasure, relationships, or dreams. Try to define what feelings you associate with the bed, and ask yourself where they apply in your waking life. You may also link a bed with sickness, or insomnia and worries.

BEES

This symbol means work, social life, or order. Dreaming of bees can also represent mass power, individual weakness, or unity of effort.

BEETLE

This insect is sometimes used as a symbol of eternal life, of fate, or cause and effect. (*see* Insect)

BEHIND

If you are left behind, it links with feelings of inadequacy. You may feel burdened with things that prevent you from being accepted by others, or feel you can't keep up with what is needed. (If the dream is about things behind you or behind something, *see* Back.)

BELL

With this symbol, ask yourself what you are being told to be aware of, or warned about.

BELLY

This symbol normally relates to vulnerability, but it is also sensual

feelings, passions, hungers, the physical side of you. Or, in a body dream, it may refer to an internal organ. (*see* Abdomen)

BELOW

If something or someone is below you, you may be feeling superior, or you are looking back on something, like your past. If you have climbed up to somewhere, then what you are looking back on is a more inclusive viewpoint.

BELT (clothing)

A belt can suggest something that restrains you, gives support, or contributes to your image in some way. Occasionally, a belt refers to protection.

BICYCLE

This suggests personal effort or motivation. A bicycle may represent your first way of gaining independence. It also links with the acquiring of a difficult skill in regard to confidence and balance. (*see* Race)

BILL

To receive a bill often symbolizes a bill of reckoning. In other words, something you have done or thought is now producing consequences that require payment. (*see* Money)

BIRDS

To dream of a bird may suggest a sense of freedom from material ties. Usually, however, the bird represents the mind and flights of fancy. It can also refer to how our minds can travel far away—in our imagination and dreams. (*see* Air)

The lifecycle of birds also illustrates some of the most powerful transitions we face as humans. Being in the nest and hatching depicts pregnancy, birth, and becoming independent. The first flight is an extraordinary thing, and is deeply felt as we struggle to exist unaided by parents—some of us never make it.

BIRTH

This represents a new beginning, a fresh start or beginning life under the influence of a new power. It may indicate the emergence of a new part of you that is perhaps difficult to coax into life. Birth dreams can also be expressions of actual infant memories of birth, with all its difficulties, terrors, and events. In this way the unconscious emotions and fears may be made conscious in order to allow us to deal with them. This may also refer to the desire to have children or your own pregnancy.

BIRTHDAY

This sign shows good feelings, recognition and warmth regarding friends, or a change occurring. Maybe it is a special time when good things or favors can come to you. Dreaming of your birthday may suggest that you are in need of attention and love. If it is someone else's birthday, it can be designed to remind you of a social obligation or a need to show affection.

Dream Fact

We spend around one third of our lives sleeping, and six years dreaming. Studies have shown that we are not switched off during dreaming—our brain waves are actually more active during dreaming than they are in waking life.

BLACK

This is the unknown, what you are unconscious of, feelings of evil, death, absence of knowledge, or the ability to see or understand. Because we cannot see in the dark, black can refer to activities that we are unaware of, or find difficult to navigate. This may cause anxiety. But black, like earth, is rich in possibilities, and has the elements of growth. (*see* Colors)

BLACKBIRD

This bird shows something, perhaps intuition, emerging from your unconscious. It can also be bad news as blackbirds are sometimes thought of as messengers of the dead. (*see* Birds)

BLAME

The things to watch for in the dream in connection with blaming are: What are you blaming someone or something else for? Define what it is. Ask yourself if you are doing this in your waking life, and how deeply you feel about the issue. How valid is the blaming? Is the blaming a way of avoiding responsibility or efforts to change? While we are blaming someone or something, we do not direct our own life. This is because blaming is like saying, "What has happened to me is all due to 'so-and-so' or 'such-and-such.' Each time this happens it does this to me." If we stop the blaming and wonder whether we can take charge of the situation, then we gain more power to change. If you are blamed: Do you feel rightly accused? If so, perhaps you are taking on unnecessary feelings of failure. You may be overly self-critical or perhaps you are not letting yourself learn something important.

BLANKET

This usually links with protection from the cold, or being alone and wrapped up in your own feelings. It can also stand for what a "security blanket" represents for a child—a feeling of security when alone. Sometimes the blanket has associations with illness, sex, or caring.

BLEACH

This can show a healing process, or the cleansing of old hurts or feelings. This can be an attempt to "clean up" your emotions or attitudes, especially if applied to clothes or pain.

BLEEDING see Blood

BLINDNESS

You may be failing to see or understand something obvious. This may reflect an inability to see something about yourself or to listen to what your intuition is telling you.

BLISTER

This represents an irritating or painful experience. It is something that has gradually hurt you over a period of time, or it can be protective attitudes.

BLOCK

This is something that is stopping you from expressing yourself easily. Tensions resulting from withheld emotions can exist in the body for years, especially in the chest, neck, and back. Try using visualization techniques regularly to get things flowing in your body again.

BLOOD

Because we usually associate blood with injury, blood in your dream mostly indicates hurt or pain of some sort; perhaps emotional pain. Blood may also signify a family connection or inherited traits. It also carries disease, so the dream may be using it to signify some danger or illness in some way. A heavy loss of blood can lead to death, so seeing bleeding can show a great loss of energy or motivation in your life. In a woman's dream it can link with monthly menstruation, but the dream will probably make this clear in some way.

BLUE

This color relates to the mind, religious feelings, or intuition. It deals with expansion, such as when we sense new ideas and views. Dark blues, however, can link with anxiety or depression. (*see* Colors)

BOAT

This often depicts how you are dealing with the ups and downs of life, with its tides, currents, and changing weather. Or perhaps the ship or boat is showing how life is dealing with you, rather than you with it. In many boat dreams the drama is actually about a relationship, what you face, what your involvement is with one or more other people. It can represent the storms or calms you meet. Therefore, in some dreams it can represent sexual adventures. Sometimes, the boat portrays the journey of your self-discovery as you investigate your unconscious. The voyage you take on it stands for your adventure into the unknown, and how you cope with what is experienced. (*see* Shipwreck)

BODY

The condition of your dream body often represents what you fear or feel about yourself, maybe unconsciously. For example, you may be frightened of illness, so dream of a sick body.

Your body, or another person's body, can represent physical existence, the process of life in your body, as represented by maturing and aging, and the potential from which your growth occurs. It can also represent an aspect of your personality, your experience, or memories. Your body in a dream can also be a graphic illustration of your hidden feelings or worries, or your pains and strengths.

A body of the opposite sex can depict your non-dominant side, the parts of you that are not given much expression.

Dreaming of a body that has been killed or buried usually refers to events of your own past, especially deeply felt emotions or struggles. (*see* Abdomen, Arms, Face, Head, Legs)

BOMB

This shows explosive emotions or fears that terrify you. Your anger may explode and do you and others damage. The bomb may also suggest anxiety about unexpected events, or dangerous emotions that are about to explode. (*see* Atomic Bomb)

BONE

This may indicate a deep hurt—you feel cut to the bone. It can also suggest inner strength. But often the bones we find in our dreams are old and indicate things from the past that we still carry with us. Another association is with death. There is often a sense of implication with the death of the people whose bones are found. This is because we have at some time denied or killed a part of our own emerging self or talents.

BOOK

This is a symbol of memories, ideas, a record or expression of yourself or others. It also links with learning or vicarious life experiences, or may be a way of escaping from the world.

BOOTS *see* Shoes

BOSS

This shows the prevailing major driving force in your life, such as ambition, desire, or love.

BOTTLE

This is often associated in dreams with the vagina. It may also connect with having resources, or whatever you associate with what is in the bottle, such as alcohol. It can also denote courage.

BOX

This shows the things you store or hide inside you, such as memories or emotions. A closed box can represent the womb or emotions you repress. Depending on the size of the box, it can represent memories or treasured experiences. (*see* Chest)

BOY

If you know the boy, your dream is probably using his image to depict the qualities you see in him. You may see him as: clever, shrewd, weak, sensitive, a thinker, or a crook. In whatever way you see him, this represents the trait in yourself. If you are a male, the boy may

also indicate yourself at that age, and what you felt and what issues you faced. If you are female, the boy can depict your growing ability to express yourself creatively, or what you feel about having a boyfriend. If you are a mother then it can relate to feelings about your son.

BOYFRIEND

This symbol shows what feelings or fears you are facing about your boyfriend. In dreams you explore not only your anxious feelings, but all your longings too. So difficult dreams about your boyfriend are usually about what you fear, not what the boyfriend will do. Dreaming about an ex-lover often shows that you have carried feelings with you from the relationship, and your dreams about him or her are trying to work out some way of feeling at ease within yourself about the breakup. This is especially true if the breakup was painful. Unless these emotions are freed from your past, they are not available to you in the present.

BRAIN

This relates to your thoughts, and intellectual faculty, your potential and creative ideas.

BREAK/BROKEN

Breaking something in your dream suggests broken promises, a break in a relationship, or a shattered hope or ideal. There may be feelings of loss or hurt attached to this. So see if you can identify these in your everyday life.

BREASTS

In general, the breast represents a giving of yourself, or your own sexual pleasure. It is an expression of female love and nurture and sexuality. To go to a woman's breast in a dream may represent an expression of the baby's desire to be fed, loved and made to feel secure, that is, a regression or reliving of infant desires. A woman expresses male sexuality through her breasts, in that she fulfills the body of the infant. It may also represent emotional security.

BREATH

Breathing equates to being alive. The condition or speed of your breathing in the dream may depict your pace of life. If you are holding your breath, this shows you holding on, staying in control. It may also suggest fear or stress. Fast breathing shows excitement or stimulation. Being under water and not breathing indicates the womb, where we existed without breathing. It is also connected with a different awareness, where there are no sexual or biological drives, and no opposites. It is usually deeply peaceful but may be an escape from reality. (*see* Air)

BRIDE

This symbol is usually connected with marriage. The dream may be exploring your hopes and desires, or your anxieties or presentiments. A bride in your dream can also suggest love, receptivity, and fertility, perhaps a desire for physical love, marriage, and children. If you are an unmarried female, then it can point to the urge to leave home. In a man's dream the bride often indicates his feelings and emotional nature. (*see* Marriage)

BRIDGE

This is a link between opposing or different emotions, desires, or directions. It can relate to coping with difficulties. Sometimes, the bridge signifies changing from one phase of life to another. It can mean leaving something behind, like youth. It can be a link between people, such as someone you love. Or it can represent work—a link between you and an opportunity.

BROTHER

This symbol probably represents your feelings about a brother. These may include rivalry, anger, feelings of persecution, love and admiration, authority, or an outgoing ability to deal with the world. If you don't have a brother, it most likely depicts either a personality trait illustrated by the dream character, or your male side.

BUBBLE

This is often used in art, literature, and dreams to represent the transience of the world, worldly ambition, and our physical life. It can depict the soul and its relationship with the eternal. The bubble may burst, but the consciousness that experienced being a body and a person remains.

BUILDING see House

BULL

The bull connects with your powerful sexual, protective, and family feelings. If you are frightened of the bull, it suggests you are anxious about your sexual drive or aggressiveness. The bull also denotes bodily or mental strength and inherited qualities or possessions.

BULLET

This can signify a desire to, or feelings of, hurt. It can be force, sexual impregnation, or the penis in its aggressive form. (see Weapons)

BURGLAR

In women's dreams, the burglar is often a fear of sexual intercourse or being entered unwillingly. In male dreams, it may be guilt about stolen love, or goods. It can be a cry from your unconscious to contact your repressed side.

BURIAL

Connected with death, burial can represent fear of personal death, or that of loved ones. It can also be an unconscious desire to see others dead or removed. But it is often used in dreams when we feel buried away from society,

or by life. Sometimes, we repress a memory, emotion, desire, or talent. Our past is buried within us. Your dream may indicate letting go of the past, of something dead, or allowed to die. The earth can also represent your mother or the past. Burial may therefore symbolize being dominated by an overpossessive mother, or the inability to break away from her. If you are being buried alive, it may be birth memories and fears.

BUS

This is something you are doing or undertaking with other people or in public. Sometimes this relates to feeling overweight. A bus stop suggests waiting for something to get you involved, or take you to where you want to go.

BUTCHER

This may denote a fear of someone's anger; or being a butcher may symbolize aggressiveness, worldly attitudes, or a lack of love.

BUTTERFLY

This is the beautiful creature that emerges from an unpromising start. It relates to vulnerable beauty or the changeless state that emerges from physical experience. It also shows transformation.

BUY/BUYING see Shop

C

CAB *see* Taxi

CAFÉ
This is about feelings of relaxation, a connection with others, or loneliness if you are alone. (*see* Bar, Food)

CAGE
This points to your feelings of frustration and perhaps anger, or even a sense of defeat or emptiness. The prison in your dreams is of your own making, created out of your attitudes and fears. So it is important to define just what you feel in the cage, and what the associated feelings are with the cage itself, and all the other people involved. (*see* Prison)

CAKE
This indicates pleasure and sensual satisfaction. It may even relate to childhood pleasure and rewards, or marriage or birth if it is a celebratory cake. (*see* Food)

CALENDAR
The calendar represents the passage of time or a schedule you need to remember. It can also be memories or intuitive thoughts of events times, or looking forward to the future.

CALF
This is the vulnerability of your babyhood, or perhaps one of your children. If you are a farmer, it may have associations to do with farming. (*see* Animal)

CAMEL
This may relate to a sterile or dry situation you are in, and your ability to deal with it. Occasionally, the camel is also associated with being pregnant, because of its hump.

CAMERA
This symbol suggests something to do with memory, the recording of impressions, or the attempt to capture a fleeting idea or experience. It can relate to noticing events or people and recording fleeting impressions. (*see* Photograph)

CANAL
The dream is probably a comment on the way you direct your emotions and energy, and what this control or decision making means in connection with your relationships and goals. (*see* River, Water)

CANCER
Any dream including the subject of cancer may connect with fear of the

illness, and in some rare dreams, a warning. But usually it links with a part of your nature or emotions that do not harmonize well with the rest of you. Therefore, they create conflict or even a threat to your well-being. If another person figures strongly in your dream, it may suggest that their influence is undermining your own well-being.

CANDLE

This often associates with the penis. It is also a symbol of wisdom, understanding, and the passage of time—your own life passing away. If you light a candle in darkness, it shows confidence and awareness of dealing with the anxieties and ignorance that can emerge in the dark. It may also indicate a birth or prayer. (*see* Fire, Light)

CANDY

This is a return to a childlike way of gaining pleasure or reward. It may link with dieting or your feelings about it.

CANNIBAL

This is the part of you that may be living off the lives or efforts of others, instead of producing them for yourself. If you are threatened by cannibals in the dream, then it is others possibly trying to live off your efforts.

CANNON

This represents the male sexual organ, and aggressiveness or destructive desires.

CANOE *see* Boat

CAP *see* Hat

CAPTIVE

This shows a fear of being bound or subject to other people, or of being trapped by circumstances in your life, marriage, or work. It can also be guilt about deeds or desires. You may be a prisoner of your own moral beliefs, ideas, opinions, or emotions, depending on the dream's context. (*see* Cage, Prison)

CAR

Many car dreams dramatically represent control, or lack of it, as you encounter the opportunities or obstacles in your life. This control is sometimes illustrated by who is driving the car, indicating whether you are taking the lead or allowing someone else to direct the relationship. But there are many other associations with your dream car, such as your energy and drive represented by the engine; your sexuality showing whether you can attract a partner by the type of car you have; your relationship by seeing who is in the car with you; your family life from an outing, and whether you are included; your body by the malfunctioning of some part of the car. The dream of crashing or being involved in a crash can sometimes be about your anxiety about driving, but it is often about the sort of difficult collisions you sometimes have in relationships or life situations, such as when you are at work. (*see* Parking Lot)

CARDS (playing cards)

These denote fate, luck, or the unexpected or unplanned events in life. They represent the skill of managing a social life and coping with what life "deals" you. Cards are sometimes associated with the devil or bad luck.

CARNIVAL

This indicates dropping social or moral restraints by letting go. It can also depict creativity, your social connections, or, alternatively, sexual opportunity.

CARRY/CARRYING

This usually suggests you possess, or are carrying, something within yourself. What it is depends very much on what you are carrying. If it is a positive living thing, can you acknowledge that you have this energy or feeling and can use it to your own benefit? If it is a dead thing ask yourself where in your body or feelings you are carrying this deadness. Why do you need to hold on to something that is not living and growing? Can you now let go of it? If it is an object, is this a useful object? Does it suggest a burden or a possibility? In what way can it be useful? Perhaps it is a waste of energy, such as old memories that are not productive. If so, can you let go of them? If it is a useful thing, what talent or skill do you have that you may not be using?

CASE *see* Bag

CASH *see* Bank, Money

CASTLE

This depicts the techniques you have developed, possibly in childhood, to defend yourself against attacks from other people. This type of defense is a way of surviving in what is often a harsh world, but in adulthood such defenses need to be reevaluated to see if they are still valid or relevant for you.

CASTRATION

This represents a fear of not coping sexually or losing sexual confidence or desire. It is to do with cutting off deeper feelings, sympathies, ambitions, and energies. To cut off the penis or testicles illustrates the action of repressing the feelings, emotions, and urges represented by them. You may deny or repress your urges through fear, because you feel guilty about your sexuality, or due to convictions that you are inferior or repulsive. The denial may also be through a dread of pain, the sort of emotional agony that arises from bad times experienced in a past relationship.

CAT

You may have felt a lot of affection for a cat, and so associate it with sensual or even sexual pleasure. It can also represent your physical need to be cared for or to care for someone. (*see* Animal, Kitten)

CATERPILLAR

This symbol shows the sort of changes we make from infancy to maturity. It is sometimes used as an image of the penis. (*see* Chrysalis)

CAVE

This is associated with a woman's sexual organs. It can indicate the womb or the experience of life in the womb, prior to birth. It can also mean contact with the past, with your inner life, or sometimes the treasures of past levels of consciousness. If there is a spring in the cave, it is a link with your core self.

CEILING

This relates to something out of your reach or above you, or something that defines the limits or extent of your mind or ambitions. This means it has a connection with your self-image and what you unconsciously feel about who you are. It can also suggest the influence of others, such as when people live above you.

CELEBRITY

Meeting or being a celebrity may show that you desire attention and acclaim. Or the famous person may be your own potential, often unacknowledged and projected onto the dream character. If you are deferring to the character or feel they have power over you, it may be showing how you relate to a parent or how you deal with feelings about your own status. If you have difficulty relating to the famous person, you may be struggling with respecting yourself or your desires, ambitions, and efforts to become successful at work. Sometimes, the person may, because of their life or role, represent a particular quality, such as courage or love, or "ruling" drives in life, such as authority, etc.

CELLAR *see* Basement, Cave

CEMETERY

You are probably dealing with thoughts and feelings about death, your family heritage of attitudes or traditions. In a few cases, the dream may be a form of contact with someone you know who is dead. The cemetery may also refer to things in your life you have "buried." It can also be about any melancholy in your life or feeling "different" from other people. Another possibility is a relationship that you think is "dead and buried."

CENTER

If it is a person or thing in the middle of something, your dream is emphasizing the importance of the thing or person. If the middle is between opposites, it suggests either conflict or balance, depending upon your feelings in the dream.

CEREMONY

Your dream is probably reiterating something that is taking place in your life. For example, at puberty your body carries you from youth to manhood or

Money dreams

Dr. Calvin Hall, along with Henry Reed, both respected dream researchers, investigated thousands of dreams from a man in Cleveland. The man had received little education, but he managed to write down his dreams each morning. He would then refer to the daily horse-racing sheets to see if he could find any connections, and place a bet on the horse accordingly. He kept a note of all bets, and the notes show hundreds of wins, and the amounts won.

However, most money dreams are indicative of how you feel about your relationship with events and opportunity. So dreaming about having money stolen, for instance, would be indicating a sense of loss. For many of us, money is connected with effort. We work a week for a week's pay. So the loss of money can also suggest a feeling of sinking, of effort expended for nothing, or resulting in no sense of security. Sometimes money can indicate the weight of responsibility, as when we have to earn enough for our keep. But the unconscious has a different view of money, seeing it as a force in nature akin to electricity. It existed before your personal life, and will be there at your death. Like electricity, it works in certain ways, and some people, understanding these ways, build up great batteries of it. Yet in itself money is nothing, just paper notes or metal coins. We create its power.

womanhood. This is an incredibly important event, yet society seldom acknowledges you as a changed person. Your dream may do this, and even reveal some of the mysterious new qualities you have as you move from one stage of life to another.

CHAIN

This relates to attitudes, beliefs, and fears that create some form of bond, bondage, or limitation. It also depicts strength or the feelings or links that bind or connect you to others, to work, a religion, or a set of ideas. A link in the chain represents the strength or weakness of one person, or of a particular attitude or aspect of your strength or linking power.

CHAIR

A symbol of passivity, rest, or a relaxed attitude. It can also suggest inactivity, receptivity, or openness, and possibly even escapism.

CHAMELEON

This indicates changing emotions, instability, or a sense of duty. Changing values are occurring to suit outer events.

CHAMPAGNE

This denotes luxury, being rich, worldly success, a celebration or a prelude to a sexual relationship. (*see* Alcohol)

CHARITY SHOP *see* Secondhand Store

CHASED/CHASING

Anything that moves toward you in a dream usually signifies that you are becoming more aware of it and feeling it more intensely. So being chased in a dream usually connotes that you are fearing something strongly and are trying to avoid confronting it. This is not usually a good policy as you can never get away from yourself. If you are chasing something, it shows that you are making an effort to gain something. Try to define in your mind what is holding you back.

CHEATING

In some way you are not living up to your real feelings about your life. Alternatively, you may be feeling betrayed, or have had your trust abused.

CHEMIST *see* Drugstore

CHESS

This shows the skills and strategies you use in meeting the circumstances of your life. It may also point to careful scheming or planning to win, or to defeat an opponent. (*see* Games)

CHEST

Sometimes, this points to a connection with your physical chest. But most often it shows what emotions, memories and passions you are storing within you—literally in your chest. You may hide precious and loving feelings too, keeping them locked up, or shut away inside you.

CHEW

This indicates you are carefully considering or experiencing something. It also links with analyzing a problem. (*see* Eating)

CHICKEN

In many cases this depicts nourishment or doing well in life. It may also refer to the female side of a male or being "chicken" or scared. The hen depicts a mothering influence. (*see* Birds)

CHICKS

This is a reference either to your own babyhood or events linked with it. It can also relate to your baby or babies. (*see* Birds)

CHILD

This symbol usually refers to youthful memories or attitudes that still live on inside you. If you become a child in a dream, you may be feeling immature in some way. The child also points to what is growing and eager in you, or what is vulnerable and perhaps easily influenced in its growth. The dream events will give you insight into what is happening to your "child" self. If this is one of your own children, look up son or daughter. (*see* Boy, Daughter, Girl, Son)

CHIMNEY

This represents the channel of female energies or libido. It can also refer to smoking, the birth canal, or inner warmth. If it is belching black smoke, it suggests the grim mechanized side of our culture, centered on commercial production instead of humanity.

CHIN

A chin represents resolve, sternness, obstinacy, or character. It is your ability to take the blows of life on the chin.

CHOKING

This is not being able to swallow or accept something. It is also an emerging emotion or memory.

CHRYSALIS

This shows an outer inactivity, while you are inwardly going through great change. It can relate to a new aspect of yourself that is getting ready to emerge, or it can sometimes be a desire to retreat from the world. (*see* Butterfly, Caterpillar)

CHURCH

This may show your religious beliefs or feelings about organized religion. It sometimes shows the sense you have of your link with all the life around you, or the lack of that awareness. It also represents orthodox beliefs or the dogma of religious organizations.

CIGAR/CIGARETTE

In some ways this may be similar to alcohol, as it depicts something that can change the way you feel. But as with alcohol, it does so at a cost. It is also habit-forming. So smoking can depict the sort of short-term stimulus and good feeling that comes from something that is potentially harmful. It can also link with dependence, anxiety, and the ways you deal with it. It relates to social contact, how positively or negatively people respond to you, or even worries about cancer. It sometimes depicts male sexuality.

CINEMA

This can be a mirroring of the dramas and passions taking place in you, perhaps unconsciously. It may be a way of exploring issues in your life. If cinemas link with romantic memories, then it can show you how to use the feelings you experienced.

CIRCLE

This connotes completeness, wholeness, and all the parts of your being: mind, body, and spirit. It also represents the universe as a whole or harmony and perfect symmetry. It sometimes symbolizes an enclosure or restraining influence or protection, or it can be the womb or female sexual organs. It may also depict emptiness, receptiveness, or a fertile condition. In some dreams you may walk in a circle, or be spontaneously moved in a circle. This means that you are enclosing, protecting, or bringing the enclosed under the power that caused you to move in a circle.

CIRCUMCISION

Dreaming of circumcision may be connected either with feelings of losing some sexual power, or of cleaning the penis. In some cases, it can indicate the memory of being circumcised.

CIRCUS

This shows the training or discipline that has been put upon your own instincts and natural feelings. The circus indicates the hoops that you have to jump through in order to survive in life or earn a decent living.

CITY

This shows your relationship with strangers, with life on the street, and your interaction with society and the many choices it confronts you with about direction, relationships, or activities. It also relates to your sense of community, along with the mental and emotional environment in which you live. It can represent a work opportunity, or just opportunity. The town of your birth depicts a familiar way of life, how you usually go about things, or the life you lived while you were young. If it is a strange town, then you may be exploring something new in your activities, possibly relationships with strangers. Or perhaps you are facing new or changing attitudes or a different way of life, new choices or opportunities.

CLASSROOM

As so many impressions are formed at school, the dream image of a classroom usually expresses something of these past experiences. It may relate to study, to your relationship with authority, or it can be about issues of performance. Think back, and try to remember what particular experiences were etched into your psyche during all those years at school.

CLIFF

The cliff represents a fear of, or the possibility of, falling in the eyes of others or yourself. It can be a fall from power or achievement, or a fear of not being able to achieve. Other meanings of this symbol can be that you are faced with the feeling of being on edge, facing danger, making a difficult decision, taking a risk, encountering a barrier or the unknown, depending on the dream's content. If you are on top of the cliff it can give you a wider view of life, one that includes death.

CLIMBING

This indicates that you are trying to overcome, or rise above, difficulties. You may be trying to achieve a new viewpoint, or to learn or develop a new understanding. Sometimes, we climb in a dream to get away from something or to get out of a current difficulty. We also climb to reach something, and in doing so may take a risk. If you are approaching middle age, climbing a hill can represent the first half of your life, and going downhill for the years ahead.

CLOCK

This may refer to your sense of connection with other people, duties, or the disciplines you place upon yourself. The clock can sometimes represent your span of life, and the ticking, your heart. It may be saying, how much time do you have left? What time of your life is it?

CLOSET

This can depict different social skills or attitudes you use in meeting people or gaining confidence. The closet may also depict feelings about a past relationship, if it is one that was in a house you shared. To be trapped in a closet suggests that past feelings or attitudes are restricting you in some way.

CLOTHES

These can often show ideas and feelings about how others see you, or how you like to be seen. Clothes also allow you to change how people relate to you so they can represent the different ways you express yourself. They may disguise what you really feel, or cover up something. Occasionally, clothes represent the attitudes you use to protect yourself or fend off other people. Underclothes, such as an undershirt or petticoat, refer to your less obvious feelings and attitudes. Armor and protective clothing refer to the attitudes you use to protect yourself against what you feel may be an attack or painful. Changing clothes shows how you can express yourself in different ways or different moods. Children's or teenage clothes in an adult's dream suggest youthful attitudes or behavior. The wrong sort of clothing is probably saying that your social behavior is not appropriate. (*see* Coat, Hat, Panties, Pants)

CLOUDS

Very often clouds appear in dreams where there are spiritual or religious feelings. If the clouds are dull, then it suggests worry or depression of some kind that is obscuring your best feelings.

CLOWN

This symbol depicts feelings of being a fool or the readiness to be a fool for the sake of love or your beliefs. It can suggest feeling foolish in your present situation, or even hiding pain under clowning behavior. The clown can also represent the irrational side of you. He can show aspects of your personality that burst out without any apparent reason, leading you to do things that are not to your advantage.

COAT
We all have different modes of behavior, and the coat, unless it is very special, represents your everyday self and the responses and attitudes you use when meeting different people. (*see* Clothes)

COCKEREL
This bird brings a warning, or indicates aggression, masculinity, or the male sex organ. (*see* Birds)

COFFIN
Thoughts and feelings about death are often in the background of your mind, and dreaming of a coffin suggests you may be exploring how you will relate to your own demise. If your coffin dream includes another person you may be subconsciously worrying about their health, or fear that you may lose them in the near future. The process inside you that produces dreams always links death with rebirth, unless you paint its face with deep anxiety or worry. (*see* Death)

COIN
Sometimes a coin has similar symbolism to a circle (*see* Circle). It can also link to feelings of worth or things you love. (*see* Bank, Money)

COLD/COLDNESS
This suggests repressed or withheld emotions, desires, and probably your

sexuality. Sometimes, it means you are feeling neglected or "left out in the cold." Occasionally, cold and coldness can be connected with feelings about death.

COLORS
In dreams, colors usually show shades of feeling, or attitudes of mind. Many people seldom dream in color, so when it appears, it is often to do with strong emotions in the dream. This is particularly true where red appears. It is therefore worthwhile defining what feelings accompany the color in your dream when interpreting it. (*see* Blue, Green, Orange, Red, Yellow)

COMB
This may be describing something you do to straighten out your thinking or to change how you appear to others. (*see* Hair)

COMPASS
This indicates your sense of direction or decision making. It may relate to expressing what is your best way forward in life, and the ability to continue when you are facing opposition and other confusing events.

COMPUTER
This can link with thoughts, but also with different aspects of the computer, such as the way we use it to enhance creativity and communication. So it can represent mental abilities or personal potential. It can also represent memory

—in particular, your extended memory and unconscious. (*see* Internet)

CONFESSION

Sometimes a confession in a dream comes from a very deep place. It may involve a great deal of truth or passionate feelings. So it is worthwhile trying to make contact with the feelings and insights.

CONJURER

This symbol may be referring to self-deceptions, or the deception of others. But it may also point to the magical abilities your unconscious has. The mind too can shift and change amazingly. It can create apparent realities out of thin air, as it does in your imagination or in your dreams. (*see* Roles)

CONSTIPATION

This represents inner tension, withholding feelings, or lack of self-expression or self-esteem. It may also be referring to a physical problem that you have.

CONVICT

The convict may be depicting your sense of meeting with a part of you that has been treated as anti-social or has not been allowed freedom of expression. In a few cases it may also represent a play on words to do with conviction. (*see* Prison)

COOK/COOKING

The cook may be illustrating practical life skills that make your life experience more palatable. Cooking may also link to motherhood or responsibility, perhaps of feeding your own family. It can also portray reproduction. If you are cooking food for someone in your dream, it can indicate you are giving yourself to someone. (*see* Food, Oven)

CORD

This sometimes suggests the weaving together of many smaller interests to one purpose, for strength. There is also a link with restriction, being tied, or even internal knots through tension or ties that are painful. Therefore, there may be some indication of a relationship being involved in the dream, along with the things that bind or tie us to other people. Breaking or cutting the cord suggests breaking with relationships that bind you, or cutting ties that have held you.

CORNER

If you are in a corner, depending on the dream, it may show you with little room to maneuver in your life or in a relationship. You may be feeling trapped or see no way out of the situation. It can also suggest a complete change of direction, a meeting, or a turning point in your attitudes or approach to something. If you are turning a corner, it can literally mean that you are undertaking a new phase in your life or are making some changes. Perhaps you are doing something that opens up a new opportunity or view of things, whether helpful or difficult, depending on the dream.

CORPSE

These are feelings or actions you have denied. For example, you may kill your love for someone if they hurt you. This can be shown as a dead body in your dreams. It can also be a feeling, such as sympathy or forgiveness, that you have deadened. You may say, "Why should I forgive them? They do not deserve it," and this attitude can prevent parts of your inner feelings from being expressed consciously. It can also represent a fear of death or a desire to see someone dead or out of the way. In a few dreams, the corpse represents feelings about disease, human vulnerability, and mortality. (*see* Death)

CORRIDOR

This suggests you are feeling in some sort of "in-between state," as can happen when you are moving from one situation to another. Occasionally, the corridor even suggests the experience of birth. If the corridor provokes difficult feelings, it may be depicting your emotions of being unable to get out of a bad situation. It may also suggest a direction produced by circumstances, or even the female genitals. (*see* White)

CORSET

This indicates sexual restraint, or holding back outer pride or vanity that does not bring inner changes. It may also suggest

being in control, or unconsciously holding yourself back and creating a social corset, for example.

COSMETICS

This indicates femininity or the mask we wear in hiding our true feelings or thoughts from others. It can be our attempts not to see ourselves as we are, or not to face facts. Sometimes, it is skin problems, or trying to improve yourself.

COUGH/COUGHING

This represents something that is felt as an irritant—a feeling, a painful memory, or something you have not expressed.

COUNTRYSIDE

This shows your feelings of relaxation, and what you are without trying. So it portrays your natural or spontaneous state, or the natural life forces alive in you. If the countryside is wild and rugged or stormy, it can suggest you are encountering a difficult time in your growth. The countryside often depicts moods. So a rainy day can suggest a quiet or slightly withdrawn mood. A sunny environment links to higher feelings of pleasure and hope. In country lanes in dreams, you often meet what is unbidden and spontaneous in you. This may be disturbing, because it may come in the form of a wolf or animal that you feel you cannot control. It is important to find some sort of working relationship with such an animal.

COUPLE

This symbol depends a great deal on the dream. It can suggest your parents, a marriage or a relationship. It is certainly about a relationship or partnership of some kind. Whether the indication is positive or negative depends on the couple in the dream.

COVER

Usually we cover something to hide or protect it. It can also link with feelings of inclusiveness or togetherness if you cover yourself and someone else. If you are covered in something, for example, dust, oil, etc., then it suggests a condition you are in that will need defining by imagining yourself in the situation and taking note of what you feel.

COW

This represents femininity, motherhood, or female sexual feelings. It can also suggest lack of intelligence.

CRAB

This symbol evokes fear or strong emotion causing tension within, especially abdominally. This may be due to fear or guilt of sensual pleasure. It may also represent outer hardness or cynicism covering inner softness, or outer hardness and greed in life. If the crab is threatening someone, it points to a desire to cause pain to others. Being nipped by a crab may indicate psychosomatic pain or illness.

CRASH

You are obviously feeling confronted by something difficult to avoid. Perhaps conflict is involved, or it may indicate an unexpected event or carelessness. (*see* Car)

CRATER

This refers to the responses left by something that hurt you in the past. It can be a memory of an old hurt, old emotion or pain, or a frightening situation. If volcanic activity is involved, then it is a deep hurt with unexpressed emotions.

CREATURES

Sometimes we dream about creatures that are not like any animal we know, perhaps they are ancient, or mixtures of plants and animals. These can represent our fear of things, such as bacteria, or illness due to micro-organisms. Occasionally, they may even represent what such an illness is doing in the body.

But frequently they point to the wonderful cellular activity and processes in your body, or the unconscious activities of the mind.

CREDIT CARD

This often links identity or social power and can represent the ability to move around and pay your way. It can link with feelings of ease and relaxation that can be destroyed if the credit card is lost or stolen, or if you are in debt. (*see* Money)

CROCODILE *see* Alligator

CROSS

Starting with its most popular uses, it can depict a trial we face in life, the cross we have to bear. It can also mean completion or finality, even death.

CROSSING

If you are crossing a road or a river in your dream, it suggests that you are making a change of some sort. The change may be in connection with a relationship or a way of life, such as moving from being single to married, or moving into employment. If there is danger involved in any way, it shows the fears and difficulties you are meeting in making the change. When you see a friend cross a river and you cannot, this sometimes indicates their death.

CROSSROADS

The crossroads relates to making decisions and a convergence of different desires, or it can be the need to choose a direction, and therefore a turning point in life. Alternatively, it may represent indecision, a fear of not doing the right thing.

CROW

This symbol shows a fear of death, bad luck, or possibly failure. A crow is known as a messenger, so it is sometimes interpreted as a warning of death, marriage, or impending important and difficult events.

CROWN

This can mean success, experiencing new dimensions of your mind, enlightenment, or it can also refer to your father if the crown is on the head of a man.

CRUTCH

This can relate to compensating for feelings of weakness, a lack of confidence or vulnerability in your personality. It can be an attitude or courage that you automatically adopt to get you around in life while you are healing from a physical injury.

CRYING

This is usually a direct expression of feelings experienced in the dream. But occasionally you can cry in the dream without knowing why, and then it usually links with emotions that you have not allowed yourself to express, and which have been pushed out of sight. If possible, it is best to let these surface.

CRYSTAL

This depicts the human sense of the eternal or your wholeness. It can also be rigid views or emotions or crystallized opinions or habits.

CUBE

This represents your physical existence. It is also linked to the number four, and stands for stability, strength, and physical expression, so therefore it also relates to the body. The square or cube is an enclosure in three dimensions, like our body, so that in its center hides a fourth dimension—the mind or our personal awareness. The cube can also indicate orthodox patterns or the establishment. (*see* Numbers)

CUP

This shows receptivity, or openness. In some way you are offering yourself or being offered something.

CURSE

This usually refers to fears that an evil influence is attached to your life. Such fears become expressed in the image of a curse. It can also point to the influence of past action and that arising from your forebears.

CUTTING

Mostly this symbol deals with how we make a break in a relationship or an activity. The ties that bind us to others and to duty are invisible but powerful, and are made real in the dream by things that might bind or link us with others. Cutting can also relate to dissociating from growth and aging. (*see* Scissors)

CYCLONE *see* Tornado.

D

DAGGER

This is a fear of being hurt or a desire to inflict hurt. (*see* Knife)

DANCE/DANCING

This symbol is a spontaneous expression of inner feelings. It can also encourage contact with the divine. If you are dancing with someone, it usually shows a loving relationship, or it can be the prelude to a new sexual relationship. If the dance seems awkward and unnatural, it shows there is a lack of harmony with your dancing partner.

DANGER/DANGEROUS

There are many things we may feel are dangerous, such as falling in love, changing employment, or moving. Your dream of danger may be showing you what you have not acknowledged is causing you anxiety. If the danger involves someone you know, it is most likely revealing your anxieties about that person, or your fears of losing them, a fear of their death or a fear of them hurting you. You therefore need to define just what the dream is portraying as dangerous. These types of dreams seldom predict the future.

DARK

This denotes a lack of understanding, something that is difficult to grasp or is obscure. Dark can also mean ancient, worn dark with age, and can relate to depressing feelings. A woman with dark hair sometimes represents intuition. Similarly, a dark-skinned person in a dream can be parts of yourself that are difficult to understand, and the obscure ways in which they influence you. Dark water suggests powerful emotions not yet defined or understood. Dark colors indicate feelings that are emanating from your unconscious, or it can be unhappy feelings. (*see* Colors)

DAUGHTER

Dreaming about your daughter often relates to how you feel about her. Is she an adventurous, creative person? If so, then dreams will usually be depicting your own feelings of creativity and risk-taking. Is she an introverted person, or anxious? Are you worried about her? If so, then the dream is either about your own urges to withdraw, or your feelings of concern for her. She can also represent what is happening in your relationship with your partner.

In a mother's dream, your daughter can represent the companionship you feel with her. She can be the image representing the difficulties you feel with her. Do you feel your daughter is competing with you for male attention? Is she representing yourself at that age?

In a father's dream, your daughter usually represents your feelings, your more feminine or receptive side. So problems in the dream can suggest you have problems allowing your feelings to develop. A daughter can also depict whatever difficult feelings you have about mistakes you have made in the relationship, or self-recriminations you experience. When she starts dating, dreaming of your daughter may also highlight your struggle of losing her to another man.

DAWN

This is the beginning of understanding, illumination, a new beginning.

DAY

This relates to being aware and active, or to a new beginning. The time of day can be important: the morning suggests the start of things, opportunities, or youth; midday indicates middle age, the central point of experience, or full awareness; the afternoon relates to the winding down of activities, the ending of things. Daylight in a dream usually depicts a particular mood: a bright day suggests positive feelings, whereas a dull day shows some despondency. A day is also a period of life that begins and ends. (*see* Night)

DEAD

Seeing something dead in your dream suggests you are realizing that some part of yourself, or your feelings, is no longer expressed fully. In fact, you may have killed that part of you by denying it, repressing or freezing it from normal life. The "death" may be related to a painful experience. But even so, it still means you have made a decision, perhaps unconsciously, to shut out that part of you. Death can also relate to a lost opportunity or potential. Dreaming of someone who is dead, a relative or a loved one, is quite common. After all, the person, such as a husband or wife, will have played a big part in your life. So their influence is still very much alive in you.

Dreaming of a dead husband or wife—Many dreams of dead people come from women who have lost their husbands. It is common to have disturbing dreams for some time afterward; or not be able to dream about the husband or wife at all; or only seeing the partner in the distance. In accepting the death, meeting any feelings of loss, grief, anger and continuing love, there are usually painful dreams. But these resolve if the feelings in them are expressed. (*see* Death)

DEAF

There may be a desire not to know what is happening to you, or something you are feeling. Or you may be frightened of hearing something that could hurt you, or to learn things about yourself that you do not wish to face.

DEATH

This is an everyday part of life. Dreams often use death to illustrate leaving something behind, such as childhood or a relationship. Also, parts of your feelings sometimes die. Our love for someone may die, for example, and so our dream illustrates this with a death, perhaps of that person. Some teenagers dream of their parents dying as they start to become independent. This is a form of killing the dependence they have on their parents as a means of growth. This can happen in some relationships too, where deep down we know we want to break free from that person.

Death is also something we sometimes create into a frightening specter. It is something we all face, so some dreams in which we die are a means of experimenting with meeting death. If we do not do this, if we are frightened of death and have not worked out a relationship with it, then we will not live daringly. But in our dream life, death usually holds in it the promise of change or regeneration. What is dead may also depict what is past. It carries traditional experience and wisdom. (*see* Dead, Illness)

DECAY

This points to something in you which is not alive, or which has been deprived of expression. It could be something you do not allow to be acted on or acknowledged. It might even indicate a part of your body needing attention.

DEER

This is the gentle harmless aspects of your involuntary or instinctive functions. It may also refer to your sensitivity that can be hurt or wounded by aggression and cynicism, or by other people's criticism. Sometimes it is used as an image of lovesickness. In a man's dream, the deer may represent a woman who he is pursuing.

DEMOLITION

This indicates the breakdown of ideas, philosophies, emotional attitudes, or established ways of life. It can also be a threat to hopes you have cherished. There can be a feeling that another person is undermining you by being critical, arrogant, antagonistic, or aggressive. It can show major changes in your inner or outer life have been, or are being, undertaken.

DEMON

This symbol denotes the things in life and yourself that threaten you. You may feel an urge is sinful, so you repress it. Your dream then presents it as a demon, not necessarily because it is devilish, but because that is how you see it. So a person who has feelings of guilt about sex may represent them as a demon threatening to possess them. A demon may also show guilt, hatred, feelings of uncleanness, aggressiveness, desire for love, and so on. (*see* Devil)

DENTIST

This may represent a fear of pain. Or it can be connected with the mouth—the things you say, your opinions, or anger. The dentist is sometimes associated with fear of sexual abuse. (*see* Teeth)

DEPARTING

This symbol suggests you are leaving an old way of life or a relationship. It may also depict a search for something new, or change. Such a departing may reflect becoming more independent of parents or a lover. If you find work or a relationship difficult, the departing may show you wanting to escape demands. It can sometimes be death, perhaps when you see a spouse walking away from you, or departing on a journey. This is not necessarily a prediction, but a confrontation with what can happen.

DESCENT

This is a regression into more youthful ways of looking at things, or it can be immature behavior. This may mean you are meeting the effects of a childhood hurt or betrayal. It can also indicate a period of depression or feeling low. In some dreams where there is intense fear, it can show an aversion to falling or descending from favor, power, or authority. It suggests coming down to earth from a more idealistic, fanciful, or visionary viewpoint.

DESERT

This indicates a lack of feeling, intellectual aridity, skepticism, or doubts. There may be uncertainty about yourself, life, or the future. You may feel lonely or worry about being deserted or having no change in your life. It can also depict a woman's infertility. It shows the wilderness that our outer lives can present to us, creating a terrible thirst and hunger for certainty and real experience of our inner being. The desert can also represent all the so-called logical, intellectual, arid opinions, beliefs, speculations, and biases we hold that bring no real satisfaction.

DESK

It may represent work, creativity, or tasks you are working on. If you use it to write letters, it can also link with communication. (*see* Table)

DESTINATION

This is where you are aiming to go in life—consciously or otherwise.

DEVIL

This relates to all those desires, ideas, habits in your life that you feel or believe are wrong. It can also be aspects of your own natural urges that you have repressed. It is all the things that you are not master of, and which can therefore influence you against your will. For example, you may not be master of anger, emotions, hungers, or ambitions, and these may lead you to do things that deep down you do not wish to do. While the results of these tendencies may seem devilish, at the same time they offer the opportunity of wrestling with them and developing strength and awareness. The anger or urges can seem as if they are strong enough to control you, so you represent them as an external force pushing you to some sort of evil. In each of us there is also the potential for creativity or destruction. This is especially noticeable when our fears are connected with illness. Such a fear, if based on imagination rather than a real cause, can still cause illness. In this sense our own mind can turn against us. Your undirected fear may be pictured as the devil or an evil entity. (*see* Demon)

DIAMOND

This is something in your experience that is valuable and lasting. Sometimes the diamond depicts the materialistic aspect of human nature.

DICE

This is something you are gambling with, or depending on chance for a result, or the situations that life deals you.

DIE *see* Death

DIGGING

Mostly this represents delving into your memories to uncover what is buried there. But it can also be self-improvement without looking back.

DINNER

This indicates satisfaction and fulfilling your needs. If shared with others, it shows your connection or relationship with them. It can also relate to gaining nourishment. (*see* Food)

DINOSAUR

This shows your present personality and body has arisen from processes and experiences that are millions of years old. The dinosaur, or a prehistoric animal, often depicts this ancient past out of which your present self has grown. The dinosaur can also depict instinctive urges.

DIRT

This represents a sense of what is unclean, or of being unclean in mind or body. We have to realize, however, that dirt is only misplaced earth, which can form the material for growing vital things. (*see* Earth)

DISAPPEARANCE

This indicates forgetting or losing sight of something, or maybe wanting to be rid of it. Occasionally, it can depict a transforming power and the magical world of the mind, where thoughts, feelings, and memories constantly appear and disappear. If so, it suggests something that is emerging from the unconscious.

DISINFECTANT

This is used in dreams to represent healing, of removing fear, or feelings of guilt and being dirty. It is sometimes linked with pain or burning as a cleansing power. So the painful experiences of life are healing, as they force attention to the cause of pain. They make us adjust, or let go of emotions, desires, and attitudes that have caused trouble, but which we would never have let go of otherwise.

DITCH

This is an unknown situation that can cause you to fall or fail. It is a hazard of which you need to be aware. If it is a drainage ditch, it can be about the way you release your feelings. The word also associates with leaving a partner, so it can link with being ditched or ditching.

DIVING

If you are not showing off or challenging yourself in your dream, then it is probably indicating that you are taking a chance, or entering something new and unknown in life, and perhaps facing some fears in doing so.

DIVORCE

This can suggest that you are angry with your partner, or that you fear for your marriage. It can also suggest a difficulty

with your feelings and intellect. Occasionally, this indicates the future, because you sense a parting.

DIZZY

This depicts losing your sense of balance in relation to others or the world. It is a fear of falling/failing, a sense of strain, or being on the edge of falling in love, out of love, or into inner consciousness. Sometimes, this image describes being in situations that are going too fast or too intensely, and require too much input.

DOCTOR

This symbol represents your healing forces. It may also be intuition or self-knowledge about the state of your body or mind. It can be your feelings about, or need for, an authority figure. It can also be your fear of illness or death.

DOCUMENT

This usually indicates an important idea, or some information that you are about to discover about yourself.

DOG

In general, the dog in your dream represents strong feelings or urges that are only slightly friendly or proper. If you have loved dogs and been loved by them, then it can depict this love, or caring, given or received. Consider the context in your dream: a dog may represent faithfulness, doggedness, a dirty dog, or unclean feelings or urges, usually sexual. It is often used to represent a person who threatens you emotionally, such as a father or marriage partner, who shouts, barks, and rages, or shows their teeth. In this case, it refers more to feelings induced by the attack. Or it can depict your own anger and aggression. The dog is generally thought of as male, while a cat is considered female. It therefore also represents male sexuality, adventure, or aggression. As a dog sees in the dark and has keen ears, it is sometimes a symbol of intuitive knowledge. It also represents instinctive life, so it shows a person who lives without much feeling or thought, like an animal. The dog may be a guide into the unconscious. (*see* Animal)

DOLL

This symbol frequently represents yourself when you were a baby, or it shows your feelings when you were young. Many dreams including a doll show it being savagely beaten or injured. In this case, it can show how hurt you felt in your own childhood, or perhaps it means you are angry and need a target that will not hit back.

DOLPHIN

The dolphin depicts the sense of beauty you may feel about the deeply natural and mysterious life in and around you. It may, therefore, show you things about life that actually come from deep within your unconscious mind. So this symbol can represent your intuitive knowledge. (*see* Fish)

DONKEY

This represents your hard working and long suffering body, or your automatic or instinctive body responses or processes. The ass or donkey may also show your body as a beast of burden, or that you are living as if you are only a working animal.

DOOR

This indicates opportunity or the openings that life offers. It also represents the possibility of entering new challenges contained within you, or the realization of new feelings, or new ideas. The door can also be a barrier that is placed between yourself and others, or yourself and life. The opening or closing of the door represents the movement of your feelings and attitudes. Death is sometimes spoken of as the other door, with birth being the first. The door also represents a threshold between one feeling or condition and another. Sometimes, it can link with your sexual feelings when you allow yourself to "open" up emotionally to a special partner or lover.

DOWN *see* Descent

DRAGON

This symbol shows parts of your sexual drive or feelings that are untamed and fiery. The dragon can also represent the power and magic of your unconscious mind. However, to get the "gold" or treasure, you have to meet and deal with those wild forces contained within yourself first.

DREAMING

To dream that you are dreaming, can mean a lack of attention to everyday affairs. It can symbolize a contact with the innermost contents of your being.

DRESS

This usually depicts your feminine qualities, and shows how these are being expressed at this time. (*see* Clothes)

DRINK

This connects with your feelings of thirsting or longing for something. It also denotes satisfying longings, emotionally, physically, or spiritually. It also shows you absorbing something, taking something into yourself. Most things have some effect on how you feel, so it points to a change in some way.

DRIVING

If you are driving, you are maybe deciding your own direction in life. Driving carelessly indicates a lack of responsibility socially or sexually and a need for more awareness. Driving without a license indicates a feeling of guilt about your way of life or social conduct. It can indicate not daring to test yourself against social standards, so you may be hiding a sense of inadequacy. When someone else is driving, you are probably being influenced by them.

DROWNING

This shows you feeling anxious about something. It usually links with strong and difficult emotions that are hard to move beyond.

DRUGS

This symbol depends on what drug appears in your dream. Take time to define what you associate with that drug. For example, you may link morphine with a way of hiding pain, ecstasy with letting go of control, and prescription drugs with various illnesses or conditions.

DRUGSTORE

This symbol possibly links with concerns about your health, or some form of healing taking place. A pharmacist may depict your own insight and wisdom about your health. (*see* Roles)

DRUNK

This can either mean you are feeling out of control, or that you are being unreasonable. It occasionally means you are filled with power from inspiration, or from a connection with a more expansive sense of yourself. If you dream of driving when drunk, this shows you out of control in your life and that perhaps alcohol is dominating you. (*see* Alcohol)

DYING *see* Death

E

EAGLE

The eagle can represent several things: it can point to the powerful, strong hunting instinct you have in business, or in being a providing parent. It can depict protective strength, a male figure, or relentless energy. Because the eagle has an far-reaching gaze, it can link with your mind's ability to expand far beyond your immediate senses and concerns. The looking back can include an overview of what you have learned. It can therefore represent an inclusive vision. Occasionally, the eagle can be threatening in a dream because the wider awareness may make you feel as if you are "carried away." Being lifted into the unknown can bring unnecessary fear. (*see* Birds)

EAR

This symbol shows you being open to your feelings and intuition. It can also indicate the existence of rumors.

EARTH

This suggests the things that are a constant background to your life, which sustain you and give form to your experiences. These include your body, the processes of life, your family or cultural background, and the basics of belief upon which you stand. But earth also depicts the past, the fallen leaves of your experience from which soil and new structures of self are built. Digging into the earth is digging into your history, and in its layers you find the story of the evolution of consciousness and your life. (*see* Earthquake)

EARTHQUAKE

This points to great anxiety. This dream often occurs when enormous personal changes are taking place, perhaps coming to the surface from the unconscious.

EATING

This indicates satisfying your needs or trying to do so. Occasionally, it refers to what your body needs to eat or avoid eating. If you are the one being eaten, it may suggest you are consumed by some passion, such as sexual desire or burning ambition. (*see* Food)

ECHO

This represents your inner response from outer action. It may suggest the effect of what you do in life, like reaping what you sow. It can also show how the importance or impact of things that are glimpsed in everyday life can be overlooked.

EGG

These are possibilities, things that can develop and grow if nurtured. They are latent abilities and tendencies, good and bad. They can also represent hopes. Eggs have been used since ancient times to represent your complete nature. In this case, it is similar to the chrysalis. The egg can represent the female ovum, and life in the womb. (*see* Chrysalis)

EIGHT

This is usually associated with generation, degeneration, and regeneration. The number eight is seen as a climax where an aspect of personality that is outworn opens up to new development. It is a sort of death or degeneration that develops the seeds of the future. It is known as the sign of death and rebirth. When you look at the symbol of the figure eight you can see that the downward loop drops and then doubles back to rise positively again. (*see* Numbers)

ELBOW

This is a support: an idea or hope that gives some help or perhaps flexibility in expression.

ELECTRICITY

In general, this symbol relates to your energy in all its aspects—mental, emotional, and spiritual. This energy, like electricity, can be positive or harmful. For example, the emotional energy of fears and long-held grief can cause illness. In some dreams, the electricity is seen as frightening or threatening. This is because there are levels of your own potential and feeling you are not handling well. You may be feeling a lot of self-criticism for instance. The electricity can also be "shocking." This suggests that some event or feelings are painful. If an electric motor is burning out, be careful about dealing with your energy and emotions.

ELEPHANT

This is the great power of the unconscious processes of life, not just in your body, but also around you. Your relationship with the elephant shows how you are dealing with this enormous force. The elephant may also connect with sexual intercourse or sexual energy.

ELEVATOR

This shows the ups and downs of life, such as a rise or drop in status or your work situation, or your emotional highs and lows. So it can suggest shifts from emotional to physical sensations, for example. Elevator dreams sometimes include strong feelings of rising sexual pleasure. So the elevator can also depict the rise or fall of such feelings.

ELEVEN

The term "eleventh hour" represents last-minute activity or last desperate efforts. It also represents strength to face

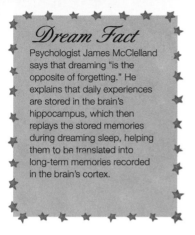

and control instincts, which gives us liberty from them. It is two on another level. Eleven is the matrix, or mold, within us, which receives and restores form after the pattern we have created or experienced in the past. (*see* Numbers)

EMAIL *see* Letter, Internet

EMIGRATION

This indicates changing habits or ideas. It is the search for self, or a change of direction in life.

END OF THE WORLD

Dreams featuring the end of the world can reflect anxiety about the future, such as many people experienced with the Cold War. Even though such a war never happened, the anxiety surrounding it dogged many people's lives for many years. End-of-the-world dreams can also show the powerful and threatening inner and outer changes that accompany major transitions. The transition from childhood to adolescence, for example, is the end of the world that existed for the individual up to that point. Such points of transition occur several times in the life of anyone who dares to grow and adapt. The end of fertility in menopause for women, the leaving home for children, the loss of a job, retirement, divorce can all be represented by the end of the world, or a world.

ENEMY

The enemy in a dream is usually a representation of our struggle with our own self-doubts, fears, and weaknesses. It particularly depicts something that is causing conflict. (*see* Shadow)

ENGINE

This represents your energy, or your heart and central drive, especially if it is a car engine. Also it can represent the life processes in the human body, all the things that run by themselves.

ENTRANCE

This represents something new happening, perhaps an opportunity or a new experience. A secret or magical entrance illustrates an attitude or a psychological "stance" that reveals a new part of yourself, or an inaccessible side. (*see* Door)

ENVELOPE

This represents the body, surroundings, protection, or a means of hiding something.

ERUPTION

This is the emergence into your waking life of processes that usually only take place in your unconscious when asleep. These powerful activities may be disturbing, but are healing.

ESCAPE

If you escaped in your dream, then you know a way to emerge from your fears, attitudes, or beliefs that are holding you back. Negatively, however, sometimes we escape from something to run from difficulties or avoid growth. (*see* Prison)

EVIL

The word evil is "live" spelled backward, as devil is "lived" spelled backward. In dreams, the sense of evil often depicts things that you have so repressed that they are no longer alive and healthy. They therefore need to be brought to the surface and expressed. In fact, they need transforming love. So frightening or shameful sexual urges, for example, may appear as demons in your dreams.

EXAM/EXAMINATION

If your dream relates to exams or being examined, it usually points to some uncertainty in yourself, or some sort of search for deeper understanding, if it is positive. If there is anxiety in the dream,

it may relate to feelings about yourself that you learned at school, due to exams and their results. If you are being examined, it can also show you looking at yourself to see who you are. If you are examined by a doctor, you may have health concerns or something that needs attention. Or, it can mean that you like being looked at and touched.

EXECUTION *see* Death, Guillotine

EXPLOSION

This may represent anger. (*see* Bomb, Eruption)

EYES

This symbol is your ability to see or realize things. Eyes also represent consciousness and knowledge, or curiosity. In such cases, this symbol often means to look at yourself. Many eyes indicate greater awareness, intuition, psychic abilities, and your innermost feelings. Looking into someone's eyes shows intimacy and understanding. Loss of sight in the right eye indicates not seeing what is going on. Loss of sight in the left eye connotes not seeing what you are feeling or having no "in-sight." (*see* Glasses)

F

FACE

In dreams the face often symbolizes an outer expression of inner or unconscious feelings. But it usually represents the part of you seen by others, whether you are aware of it or not. It can also mean you are faced with something, or are confronting something.

FACTORY

If you work or have worked in a factory, then this symbol links with your feelings and experiences of that time. The factory may also suggest industry and productivity, or the working of your body's processes.

FAILURE

Often a sense of failure arises in a dream because you have been comparing yourself in some way. Therefore, it is helpful to consider exactly what the comparisons mean or provide. You may also have experienced some competitiveness. Another thing to consider is whether the failure in the dream was "because" of something. In other words, did it happen because you took a wrong direction, or because you went along with a particular person? In this case, try to define what the "because" factor is in your everyday life.

FAINT

This suggests losing energy and enthusiasm, or feeling overwhelmed by a situation or relationship. (*see* Dizzy)

FAIRGROUND/FAIR

What you are experiencing at the fairground shows your feelings about the enormous range of differences and activities you observe in human society. It therefore depicts the range of human circumstances: from rich to poor people, midgets to giants—it shows you the "swings and roundabouts" of life. A fairground can also suggest a colorful façade. (*see* Carnival, Market)

FAIRY

This represents natural forces or processes, such as electricity, gravity, cohesion, magnetism. The unconscious tends to express such forces pictorially as images.

FALL (autumn)

This usually refers to memories; the autumn of one's life, or old age.

FALLING

Most often this symbol illustrates some threat that has arisen in your life from such things as uncertainty, loss of a relationship, money, work, or death of a close contact. What happens in the dream illustrates your drop in confidence, or your feelings of falling from power, grace, or love. Maybe you have lost confidence and so get the sinking feeling of the fall. It can even suggest falling in love, the fear of not being in control, or the wonder of "free fall." (*see* Stairs)

FAMILY

The meaning of this symbol depends enormously on what your relationship with each member of the family was or is. There can be everything from loving support to brutal arrogance. And then each person has different characteristics. So the dream content will help define this. But to generalize, the family represents the many things you learned or that are engraved on your nature from exposure to life in and with your family. Many of these things are still active in the way they influence your responses and decisions. So sometimes a family member represents one of these responses. (*see* Brother, Father, Mother, Sister)

FAMOUS PEOPLE *see* Celebrity

FARM

This usually has to do with your relationships, with your natural urges— the basic drives that motivate you, such as sex, survival, social hierarchy, parenthood, or the more down-to-earth side of yourself. It can also represent the area of your basic animal tendencies or emotions, where territorial fighting or perhaps fighting over a mate are expressed. Seeing yourself as present in a farmyard can also represents efforts to deal with all your sensual, aggressive, or animalistic urges.

FASTING

This symbol indicates withdrawal or turning away from your natural urges or it can also be not taking in what society is offering you.

FATHER

This figure represents the feelings you have about your father, the characteristics in your nature that have arisen from this relationship, or an authority figure. He can also be a teacher or someone who greatly influences you. Alternatively, he can show your own positive, protective qualities: how you relate to the "doer" inside you, your physical strength and protective qualities, your will to be. The negative aspects of the father figure are introverted aggression, dominance by fear, uncaring sexual drive, or feelings of not being loved.

FEAR

To feel fear in a dream means that you have not yet developed abilities to cope with whatever symbol is causing the fear. One of the wonderful things about dreams is that if you work with them, they gradually show you how to deal with the parts of your personalty that need to grow or heal. They show you how to meet the parts of yourself that need release, or to be understood or re-evaluated. If you persist in trying to meet all your fears, then your dreams will gradually take you on an inner journey to increase your emotional strength. You will be able to face your fears more readily, and in fact gain some power and instruction from them. You can do this by meeting each of the dream situations that involves anxiety using visualization techniques to work through what is being shown to you.

FEAST *see* Food

FECES

Occasionally, this symbol indicates something you have produced and created, something visible that has come out of you. It also suggests the corruptible parts of human nature that become manure for new growth. Feces can even represent money, riches, or fertility. In another sense, to pass feces with feelings of relief means to get rid of worries, tension, or sexual repression. To be covered in feces may suggest a fear of being outwardly repulsive, or to harbor self-destructive thoughts and feelings. To play with feces suggests a return to infantile behavior, but it may develop in the dream into a question of what to do with them or how to use them. This is

the beginning of using our basic earthly nature to creative ends, and to shaping and developing our inner self.

FEET

Your feet depict your contact with reality, your foundations. So observing what is happening with your feet in your dream will show if you are "grounded" or not. Walking with bare feet can suggest either that your path in life is more difficult at the moment, that you are more in contact with the situation you are in, or that you are suffering some impoverishment. At times, the foot can depict beliefs which underpin your actions, your basic feelings, and so on. It can also show your direction—the way you are going. Kissing the foot shows it as a symbol of lowliness, earthiness. Putting your feet up depicts the meaning of labor or work.

FEMALE

Seeing a female in dreams often represents the more feeling, intuitive part of yourself. If it is someone you know, she probably symbolizes your opinions and feelings about her, or what emotions she has led you to feel. (*see* Girl, Woman)

FENCE

This indicates a barrier, or a difficulty felt in yourself. It is either something that bars your progress or expression, or it is used as a protection from things outside yourself, or from things getting at you. If you are sitting on the fence, it shows you attempting to avoid a decision or action. In many dreams a fence or wall also suggests social barriers, the attitudes and feelings people express to keep others at a distance, to keep a separation between those of different social, religious, or economic opinions. This sort of fence may also depict tension or conflict, as was expressed by the Berlin wall that was built between two opposing powers.

FEVER

This can be a sign of bad health, or a symbol of great stress and intense emotion that is burning out its own causes and getting rid of the worries or insecurities that produced it.

FIELD

This shows your feelings of relaxation, or your natural feelings. Fields also suggest freedom from social pressure, and the feeling you have about yourself when away from other people, with your own natural inclinations. A field can refer to an area of activity, or a particular aspect of your life. If the field is in bright sunshine, or it is overgrown, then it may suggest a particular state of feeling.

FIGHT

This generally expresses angry feelings that you may have been holding back when awake. But, like a war scene in a

INSTANT INTERPRETER

Anything that transports you, such as a truck or train, shows your ability to get somewhere in life, to motivate yourself and others. Who you travel with reveals what attitude you have to those who share your endeavors. And "breakdowns" are just that—the fears and feelings that interrupt your journey.

dream, it can also point to an area of conflicting feelings or interests that you are harboring. Occasionally, a fight can express feelings not so much of aggression, but of the struggle for what is right for you—a fight or battle for your "space," or a fight against urges in yourself or influences coming from other people. This can also indicate a fight for independence. (*see* War)

FILM *see* Cinema, Movie

FILM STAR *see* Celebrity

FINDING

This is the realization of something, such as when you find the solution to a problem. It can also mean change, perhaps finding a new direction or relationship. Sometimes what you find is a clearer realization of your own identity or qualities, or facets of yourself that can be nurtured and developed.

FINGERS

This suggests how you manipulate things. We also use fingers to indicate things. Fingers are also what we grasp objects with, so they indicate our hold on people and objects. In many dreams, fingers are also involved in sex play or even represent the penis. If it is the wedding ring finger, then it can depict your marriage or state of it.

FIRE

This indicates burning love, fiery passion, emotional fever, pain, or purification. Fire is a tremendous energy that we learn to use even when quite young. So it can refer to how you use powerful emotional energies that can support or destroy. Therefore, fire can show an emergency or a sudden and difficult change. Like all energies, fire can warm, produce power, purify, and bring about chemical change, or it can consume, destroy, injure, or run amuck. It is therefore often used as a symbol for your relationship with your own powerful energies—sex, anger, ambition, and fear. Fire can also stand for suffering of a mental or even physical nature. Or it can depict the destruction of things, as happens when you are angry. Standing in or being in flames, can therefore suggest either purification, the burning out of old attitudes or experiences, or deep personal suffering. Sometimes, fire can give you advance warning of illness.

FIREMAN

This represents those of your qualities capable of dealing with your energies, burning desires, or emotional emergencies. (*see* Roles)

FISH

A fish represents the living processes of thought and feeling that go on under the surface of your mind. To fish is therefore to seek and bring to light your inner feelings or transforming realizations. Fishes depict the ideas, feelings, treasures, or sustenance of our inner, unconscious life. To be swallowed by a fish, similar to Jonah and other legendary heroes, represents a period of deep and sometimes difficult introversion.

You can also fish for compliments or information. Or something can be fishy, not quite right. Fish can also have a sexual significance and may represent fertility, prenatal experience, or life in the waters of the womb. A woman's dream of a fish or many small fishes in a bowl or small tank can sometimes represent pregnancy.

FISHING

This suggests someone who creates a receptive state of mind that allows usually unconscious insights or processes to become known. You can also "fish" for ideas, compliments, or information. A fishing rod can indicate male sexuality, personal power, or feelings of impotence. But if you love fishing, it can of course simply mean relaxation. In general, the rod is a sign of pulling something out of the unknown.

FIST

This usually shows anger or the personal strength of grasping or holding. It can also depict tension or restrained feelings.

FIVE

In the same way that the five-pointed star is similar to the human body, five has come to represent human consciousness in the body, and the hand. Sometimes, it is called the number of marriage because it unites all the previous numbers—1+4 and 2+3. It also connects with the five senses. The alchemists called it quintessence, because it arises from the other four elements—earth, air, fire, and water—and the four aspects express themselves in a fifth quality: life and consciousness. (*see* Numbers)

FLAG

This symbol depends on your feelings and connections with the particular flag. Sometimes, a flag can be seen as a warning.

FLAMES

Similar to the process of life, flames consume in order to exist, so the flame can represent your own life energy. It can also represent a spark or flame passed on from one person to another, as a candle lit from another. This suggests an influence, something ignited in you from

another person. You can also have an "old flame," meaning a past lover. Flames therefore depict the mystery of life, or self-awareness, passed from one person to another, in the same way as culture itself is passed on. (*see* Fire)

FLOATING

This symbol often appears in dreams where the dreamer is getting close to someone of the opposite sex, if some aspect of sexual feeling is present. It can show how you can go beyond the usual boundaries of your beliefs and physical senses. Floating on water suggests that you are deeply relaxed, are being indecisive, or that you are allowing yourself to be carried along by events. (*see* Flying)

FLOOD

This represents powerful and difficult emotions that are making you feel swamped and threatened by their intensity. The flood can, of course, be a release of positive feelings, such as love or affection. In any case, floods can enrich your growth if they are handled well. In many dreams about a flood the dreamer is anxious about showing and displaying positive energy.

FLOOR

This shows your support system or your physical life; how you can be floored or overcome by events that happen to you. Lying down on the floor and finding it difficult to move represents being overpowered by intense life experiences or your present situation or your environment. For instance, seeing a first floor or second floor can suggest a different situation where the dream's events are actually taking place.

FLOWER

This symbol shows growing or the growth that is going on, the opening out of your abilities or feelings, in the same way that a flower opens from a bud. Flowers can also indicate a type of spiritual energy, such as the Chakras of Indian philosophy. The context of the dream is also very important as flowers can also represent a sense of beauty or love. They are used to express warm feelings, such as giving red roses to a lover; they can also relate to sexual activity as the act of losing your virginity is called deflowering.

FLYING

This can have many meanings, depending on the dream. It can indicate that you are flying or fleeing from something that is difficult to face. This is usually an aspect of your life that you avoid by using distractions, such as your social life or media entertainment. You can also become over-idealistic, religious, or live in a fantasy world. If you are flying you do not have your feet on the ground, so it can suggest either that you have found a positive expression of your energy, or

that you have lost a practical grasp on what is happening.

Flying is positive when you are not fleeing from something. It indicates independence and the ability to deal with your emotions or fears. This type of flying suggests the desire to rise above things, to attain greater heights, to break free of limiting or cultural viewpoints. Freud explained all flying dreams as showing sexual desires, representing intercourse, or life in the womb, which in some cases is true. But flying also represents ambition, abstract thoughts, and the ability to rise above your fears. Flying in a plane or alone can be an attempt to gain insight into your future or your potential. From the air we can see forward and back. We can quickly review where we are heading, and work out the best possible direction in which to go.

FOG

This relates to uncertainty, mental ignorance, or an inability to see ahead or understand. It also represents inner mental stagnation. It can show you weighed down by too many intellectual queries, doubts or objections. It may also show your desire to hide your real motives behind a fog of self-deceit.

FOLLOWING/FOLLOWED

Whatever you are following in your dream indicates that you are being influenced by what you are pursuing or what you are looking for, depending on the dream's content. If you are being followed, this may show who or what you are influencing, or what is coming into your life. It can also be some aspect of your life that you are avoiding.

FOOD

This symbol can represent anything you depend on to sustain or strengthen you mentally or physically. To eat excessively may represent a hunger for affection, self-confidence, sex, or recognition. It may hide a fear or feeling of loneliness and emptiness. It can also connote the things you experience. In eating, you digest what you take in, so food can show what you are taking in emotionally, intellectually, or physically. Your reaction to what you eat shows what is happening to you as you absorb the food. Something might sicken you, for example, or make you strong. Food is the building material of the body, and can be the symbol for experience—the actual building material of your personality or mind.

Food or eating plays a large part in the ceremonies of many religions throughout the world. This is because it portrays your connection with the rest of life, your total involvement with creation. So eating food in this way acknowledges this communion with life and how you commune with other humans. (*see* Eating)

FOOT *see* Feet, Left, Right

FOREIGN COUNTRIES *see* Abroad

FOREST *see* Jungle, Tree, Wood

FORTRESS *see* Castle

FOUNTAIN

This is the flow of life that exists within you. It can also be an influence that springs from deep within that can satisfy your overall needs, or cleanse any negativity, and possibly heal you.

FOUR

The symbol of four is the square or cube, representing stability, earthiness, strength of a physical nature, permanency, or how you make things happen in your life. It is the symbol of the four points of the compass; the four elements—earth, air, fire, and water; the four functions—sensation, feeling, thinking, and intuition. Four, perhaps depicted as a square, often shows a sort of physical harmony in your body, or indicates a feeling or sensation of being complete. (*see* Numbers)

FREEWAY

This symbol shows the more direct approach to your goals. If the freeway appears to be blocked, then it may indicate feelings of frustration or things at the present time that are blocking your energy.

FRIEND

Friends are deeply important to us, and a dream friend can represent the important factors that a friend represents: emotional and economic support and the sharing of love and interests. But friends also represent your human state. So they will represent whatever characteristics that friend displays, far example, generosity, caution, courage, anxiety, sexuality, shrewdness, and so on.

FROG

This symbol reveals the processes that led you to transform from a tadpole/sperm into an air-breathing frog/adult. The frog is therefore a guide into your unconscious world. It is here that many unknown processes are at work.

FRONT

This symbol relates to what you are aware of, what other people see about you, or what you are doing. This has the same meaning, whether it is the front of a house, a car, or yourself. It is the "front" or façade you use when you meet other people or encounter situations. It is also the part of you that takes most of the impact from relationships and events.

FROZEN

This represents repressing your emotions, and possibly becoming cold emotionally and sexually, to be unfeeling, sometimes in a painful way. It can also mean you need affection or warmth.

FUEL

This indicates drive or motivation, or whatever has "fuelled your drive."

Basically, it refers to energy and resources. But the energy may be dangerously explosive, and this may be symbolized by gas/petrol.

FUNERAL

This can reflect concerns about death, perhaps because someone close to you has died. Death is an important aspect of your life, and dreams use a funeral to explore the subject and find greater completeness and healing. Sometimes, we dream of seeing someone we know buried when we want them out of our life. Very occasionally we dream about the funeral of a close relative or friend because we have a premonition of their death. It is a common dream to watch your own funeral. It not only allows you to define what you want to do before you die, but it also shows what you feel about death. Often this is greatly healing. Such a dream may also be a cry for attention or sympathy. If you see yourself being buried, you may be leaving behind an old way of life or part of your personality. (see Death)

FURNITURE

This is your inner contents: your beliefs, opinions, and attitudes. If the furniture is from an old home, it relates to things you felt, or a relationship you were in at that time. It relates to domesticity—the disciplines and restraints you use in a relationship or in your home life. (see Bed, Chair)

G

GAMES

These often indicate your skill in dealing with life and relationships. But similar to life, some games are dangerous and some hold good rewards. Such games as tennis are especially associated with relationships, and they can indicate superior/inferior feelings too. So the game being played may well be a way of exploring what is a useful stance to take in your life situation, or in a sexual relationship.

GANG

This shows a meeting with your fears. It may represent aggressive tendencies, or parts of yourself, and may also suggest your particular need to conform to a group or follow a leader.

GARBAGE

This is the unwanted aspects of your own memories or self, the things you want to get rid of, the things you don't like or of which you are ashamed. It is your discarded ideas or opinions.

GARDEN

This symbol reveals what you are doing with your latent possibilities. It is pointing out whether you have cultivated your abilities or buried them.

A garden is sometimes a place of love in a dream. In which case, it can connote what is growing or dying in your relationship. Another garden theme is connected with activities we do in the garden, such as playing with pets or gardening chores. The pets show what is growing in the area of your natural urges, and the gardening represents what you are doing there that is visible socially. (*see* Digging, Pool)

GARDENING

These are activities or attitudes that lead to personal development and the flowering of your potential or abilities.

GASOLINE *see* Fuel

GASPING *see* Asthma

GATE

This can be a barrier or boundary, possibly the feelings that keep us out of someone else's garden or house. The opening and closing of such a gate points to the feelings of permission or refusal we give ourselves. It may also refer to the boundary or gate between the conscious and unconscious mind. If it is open it allows selected memories to penetrate, while a closed gate prevents a massive flooding of impressions. The gate can also symbolize the passage from one part of life, or level of maturity, to another. Therefore, to stand before adolescence, parenthood, or death may be shown as facing a gate in a dream. (*see* Door)

GEESE/GOOSE

This shows freedom, your soul, wanderlust, foolishness, or group conformity. Sometimes, the goose is a symbol for a lifelong relationship.

GENIUS

This may represent feelings of inferiority or superiority. In the positive sense, it depicts your potential.

GERMS

These indicate an anxiety or unconscious worry, or something invisible that is damaging your health. Depending on the dream, the germs or virus may suggest that you are absorbing a bad influence from another person. You may also be fearful about your health, or know intuitively that you are getting an infection. Sometimes it suggests "dirty" feelings that are disturbing you about something that you have done or in which you are involved.

GHOST

A ghost represents an old memory, an old fear, or something from the past that haunts you or comes back to you. It may suggest guilt, a fear of death, intuitive knowledge, dread of the unknown, or

things that you have done or tried to bury and forget. Occasionally, the ghost is a contact with the dead.

GIANT

If you are the giant, then it may mean that you have feelings of power over others; it may also suggest that you feel inferior and that you are making compensations. If someone else is the giant, then it may symbolize your relationship with them, and may indicate feelings of inferiority, lack of power, or fear. Try to understand what the other person signifies. Apart from their size, they may represent one of your emotions, fears, or ambitions that have become too big for you to handle and have increased to giant proportions. A giant in a dream can also depict feelings you had about parents who in your childhood were giants, physically and emotionally.

GIFT

If the gift is from someone you know, it shows what you are receiving from that person in the way of support, love, or understanding. The gift itself will define what this is and if you want it. If you are giving a gift, then you are giving yourself in some way. In some dreams when a woman receives a gift, it can point to pregnancy.

GIRL

A girl usually represents your feelings, young sexuality, or vulnerability. But it depends what age you are and what gender. If you know the girl, it most likely points to her most pronounced characteristics active in yourself. If you are a male, it can refer to feelings about a sister or to your emotions. If you are a female, it can be depicting your sister if you have one, or yourself at that age. Dreaming about a young woman with your man suggests that you are worried about how lovable you are, or you have suspicions about his fidelity.

GIRLFRIEND

This symbol can reflect concerns, feelings, or issues promoted by your relationship. An ex-girlfriend in your dream suggests the feelings, difficulties, or hopes you are left with from the relationship. Alternatively, it can be the positive things gained.

GIVING

The art of giving and receiving is fundamental in any relationship. You can give time, support, money, sex, and information. So giving in a dream usually indicates some sort of relationship. But you need to define who or what is in the relationship and what is being exchanged. This will clarify what you are giving, receiving, or rejecting. (*see* Receiving)

GLACIER

This may point to emotions that are frozen in a past attitude. It can also relate to an old hurt that has never healed.

GLASS

This is the unseen but evident barrier that we often encounter in daily life. For instance, the social taboo against walking in the street undressed.

GLASSES

This is your ability to "see" or understand something clearly. The glasses may suggest a way of dealing with your difficulties in how you appear to others.

GLOVE

This symbol indicates being insulated against the world. It may be an invitation, like a dropped glove or handkerchief. It can also indicate a hand that does not have any life in it. Sometimes it means protection, or avoiding contact, or something that does or does not fit in some way. (*see* Clothes)

GLUE

This represents feelings, a sense of duty, or love or fears that keep you "glued" to a partner or job, for example.

GNAW

If you see a rat or mouse gnawing away at something, it indicates that you are dealing with or processing a worry of some sort, something that keeps attracting your attention. If there is gnawing at a bone or food, it suggests attacking a problem or situation, or it can also link with a hunger for something. (*see* Eating)

GOAL

This represents your aims and ambitions. The goal may also refer to the purpose of your unconscious drives. There can also be a link with winning (success) or losing (failure), such as in a sport.

GOAT

This symbol often depicts foolishness or the urge to break out. It can also refer to argument or "head butting," and can refer to being consumed by sexual urges.

GOD

There are many possibilities with this symbol. It may refer to a set of emotions that you use to deal with anxiety. For example, you may have a belief that a higher power is in charge and that you are okay in the world and can escape responsibility. It may also be a parent image from early infancy, or it can refer to a set of moral or philosophical beliefs you hold, such as self-judgment or something/someone you worship. It can equally be a sense of the collective awareness that lies at the deepest level of human consciousness.

GODDESS

If you are a woman dreaming about this symbol, it is most likely about your potential as a female or the connection you feel unconsciously with women as a whole. It also depicts the power of love and life that can have a transforming influence in your own and other people's life. If you are a man dreaming of a goddess, you may be connecting with your feelings as a child about your mother, or confronting the power of a woman's passions and creativity. It often deals with your ability, or lack of it, to love and meet the full flood of a woman's sexuality and longings.

GOLD

This indicates attitudes or parts of your character that are of great value. It also suggests something that does not tarnish or change with time, or something that relates to the changeless part of you.

GORILLA see Ape

GOWN see Clothes

GRADUATION

This suggests the tests you meet and the skills you develop in life and relationships.

Dream Fact

Newborn babies sleep around 16 hours a day and spend at least half of that in dreaming. With premature babies, the percentage of dreaming sleep is even higher—around 75 percent. Similarly, unborn babies spend most of their time dreaming, and this gradually diminishes after birth.

It also represents achievement, an entrance into a new life, the gaining of adulthood, or the skill leading to adult independence.

GRAVE/GRAVEYARD

This tends to indicate your thoughts and feelings regarding death. It may relate to your family's attitudes or traditions. Sometimes, but not often, such a dream is about contact with the dead. But more frequently it relates to things in your life that you have "buried." It can also refer to melancholy feelings about life or feeling "different" from other people. It can even be a relationship that we think is "dead and buried." (see Burial)

GRAY

This suggests a serious attitude or lack of vibrancy. It is sometimes associated with business: worldly activities lacking human warmth. The idioms "gray world" or "gray area" depict the way dreams use the color. (see Colors)

GREEN

This may indicate a process of positive change or some kind of personal growth. Strangely enough, this color is often found in dreams about peace and heaven. This suggests it is linked with feelings of relaxation and well-being. When dark green appears, this may refer to negative intentions or depressive attitudes—even sickness, envy, or jealousy. (see Colors)

GREENHOUSE

This can depict the tender, growing parts of yourself or others, or perhaps overprotected things.

GRENADE see Bomb

GROOM

In a woman's dream seeing a bridegroom may express the desire to be married, or to find a loving partner. It may depict feelings about the man you want to marry, or show a move toward merging with your inner and outer capabilities. In a man's dream, the bridegroom mostly shows feelings about marriage, or an attempt to integrate both the conscious and unconscious.

GROUP

This shows how you feel about being one of a crowd, and the strategies you use for dealing with a group. For example, you may be a follower, a leader, an introvert, or an extrovert.

GUILLOTINE

This is a very graphic image of losing your head, or being cut off from feelings or the body's needs. (see Body, Head)

GUN see Weapons

H I

HAIR

This symbol occurs a great deal in dreams, as head, face, or body hair. Head hair usually represents your character and gender. The style, length, even the hair color suggests the different mental attitudes, characteristics, strengths or weaknesses being portrayed. Hair can also represent your thoughts and intellectual life, or the transformation of sexual feelings into sympathy, fraternal love, protectiveness, or union with the life process. If the hair is growing on unusual parts of the body, it often shows an emerging of your natural and instinctive feelings.

HAIRDRESSER

There may be a question in your mind of how you can change the way people see you. It may also link with attention to the way you think, or how you appear. (*see* Hair, Roles)

HALL

This indicates a point of unity, a coming together of things, or a connection with new people and ideas. It can also represent an important change, such as occurs when getting married, or achieving social acclaim.

HALLWAY

The hall or passage in a house may depict how you relate to other people, or how much you let them into your life. It may also suggest the connections between the different parts of you, such as different interests or talents. Occasionally, the hallway in a woman's dream indicates her vagina.

HAMMER

This suggests power of a material or physical nature. It is the threat of aggression. It may also refer to the male sex organ, or sexuality in its physically, forceful, unsympathetic aspect. Or a hammer can express your desire to make something secure.

HAND

This relates to your deeds, outer creativeness and power in the material world. It represents what you do outwardly. So you can have a helping hand, or it may be a grasping, wringing, or heavy hand. It also depicts self-expression—how you relate to life, your ideas, opportunities, people, your children, or situations. The hand is your extension of power, it is your ability to give, take, wound, heal, support, or to do something.

Losing a hand can suggest not being able to do or create something, or to express yourself positively. If you are right-handed and it is your right hand, then it is the loss of ability to do things externally. If it is the left hand, then it represents a loss of confidence, or the ability to support your enthusiasm to act. (Reverse the context if left-handed.) (*see* Fingers)

HANDBAG *see* Bag

HANGING
This relates to anything that hangs and its meaning depends upon the thing it is hanging by or from. So hanging in a dream shows a condition of depending for support on whatever is shown in the dream. It can also indicate connection or having a hold on something. If it is a person who is hanged, it suggests the awful repression of self-expression to the point of feeling dead or depressed.

HARE
This symbol indicates your intuitive abilities, your hardiness in life, or the irrational side of your character. (*see* Rabbit)

HAT
This is your mental attitude or opinions; your thoughts, philosophy, reasoning, or logic. It can be your different ways of thinking or even the different roles you take in life. The hat can also associate with roles, as with the hats worn by a police officer or baker. (*see* Clothes)

HAUNT/HAUNTED
Usually these are memories or wounds from the past that continue to cry for your attention, or influence you in detrimental or disturbing ways. If you are doing the haunting, it suggests you are unconsciously projecting feelings or wishes toward others, or have powerful connections with people or places that need to be dealt with.

HAWK *see* Eagle

HEAD
You can lose your head, have a head for figures, or use your head. Usually in a dream, it relates to your mental astuteness, your intellect, or thoughts. But it is also often your attitudes and decision making. It also represents consciousness, awareness, or your controlling factor. (*see* Face)

HEAR/HEARING *see* Ear

HEART
Mostly, dreaming of the heart represents your emotions and longings. But it can simply depict your sense of self. It also represents inner feelings, secret thoughts, or your conscience. You can take heart, and so carry on through difficulties, or lose heart and give up. In some dreams, the heart stands for worries you may have about your health. It may not mean that you have heart problems, but simply indicates that because of feeling down, your "heart" is not in

what you are doing, so you have no zest for life.

HEAT

This symbol is about strength of feelings, passion, pressure, or a link with your state of health.

HEAVEN

This may suggest you find life difficult—if so, this is a compensatory dream. It may also be intuitive feelings about life after death, a retreat from life, or a meeting with your religious concepts, or even being in love or feeling deeply happy.

HEIGHT see High

HELL

This represents difficult feelings about life and the world that you create out of your own fears and anxieties, or from anger and malice, jealousy, etc. Sometimes, it represents the fires of pain arising from past trauma and the connected feelings. People who have suffered birth trauma often see this in a dream as hell.

HEN

This suggests motherly feelings, or it can be something to do with being female or caring for the young. (see Chicken)

HERO/HEROINE

This suggests the courage to face or wrestle with problems or trials. You are the hero or heroine of your own life. It is you who face all the difficulties and heartbreaks, you who must develop all the powers and skills of survival.

HIDDEN/HIDING

This symbol usually means the avoidance of something, such as feelings, or an awareness of something. But it also connects with not wanting to be seen or be involved. You can also be protective, or you can be hiding how you really feel about someone, or about your sexual feelings concerning a person. If you are hiding a body or object, it can be that you are not facing up to difficult feelings about them. Hiding from something dangerous or concealing a dangerous thing shows you are feeling threatened either by unconscious content or by an exterior situation.

HIGH

Sometimes, if you are located high up in a dream, this shows you having a wider grasp of your life situation. Alternatively, it may also suggest feeling isolated and distant. If something is higher than you, it can indicate feelings of awe, or a sense of being in over your head, or it can mean something more powerful.

HIGHWAY

This is the direction you are pursuing. Each direction cannot help but lead you to a particular point in your life. Much of your destiny is created by your own decisions and predispositions. A road can symbolize any direction you have taken, or are thinking of taking. It may concern where a love affair, a marriage, or a business will lead you. In the dream you are looking at the possibilities of these roads and where they go. The condition and size of the dream road illustrates your views on the routes you have taken. (see Alley, Crossroad, Freeway)

HILL

This symbol depends on whether you are going up or down the hill. If you are going up, then it represents a challenge or a difficulty to be surmounted or avoided. The summit of the hill depicts your ability to gain a more inclusive view of where you stand in life and what possible directions you can take. Going down the hill can suggest things are easy, or conversely that events are taking a turn for the worse.

HOLDING

This is a complex symbol. It may be that you are trying to control something, for example, when you hold your breath. You may be trying to control how you feel about someone or something. Holding something lets you manipulate or create something. So you need to define if what you are holding, or the way you are holding it in the dream, has this quality. Are you trying to protect something or someone by the process of holding? Or are you holding in a possessive way? This may mean an attempt at ownership and

not sharing. Is the holding a sign of responsibility, such as when you hold a baby? Or are you holding someone and expressing tenderness?

HOLE

This represents an error you may fall into, a difficulty you are facing, or a danger that confronts you. A big hole may suggest a descent into the unconscious or memories. A hole, especially with grass, foliage, or bushes around it, can represent the vagina. A hole can also be an escape route, so you need to define whether this is true in your dream. Holes in clothes or objects suggest faults, weaknesses, or even an illness. If the holes are in your body, ask yourself what personal weakness is being looked at.

HOLIDAY *see* Vacation

HOME *see* House

HOOK

This is something with a catch in it. You can be hooked on drugs, drink, or even love for someone, or you can hook on to a good idea or useful opportunity. It can also suggest a question that is being posed.

HORNS

This suggests protective strategies, or the desire to hurt. It can also represent the animal in the human.

Relationship dreams

Most dreams about relationships dramatize the dreamer's own feelings, and how they are influencing the relationship. Patterns of relating, and our confidence in love and being loved, arise in our earliest childhood. So dreams of relationships often use a child in the dream to illustrate how early feelings of need, of feeling unloved, disrupt present relationships. To understand a dream in which you are relating to others, ask yourself what situation it is dramatizing.

HORSE

The horse is a beautiful symbol that is found throughout human history, in all arts, and unconscious experiences. Basically, the horse represents instincts, energy, sexual desires, but also drives that have to some extent become "tamed" or directed. If the horse is wild and without a rider, it shows that these energies are strong enough to express themselves, despite the anxiety of your thoughts or moral conscience. If the horse is ridden, then it means such energies are being directed. But sometimes dreams suggest that although a horse is being ridden, it needs free rein, indicating excessive conscious control of your feelings, and the need to slacken your hold on yourself.

HOTEL

This suggests new areas of yourself. It can be attitudes or a situation that may not be permanent. It can show luxury and ease, or a state of mind or being in which you are lodging, vacationing, or passing through on your way to somewhere else.

HOUSE

This usually represents yourself, and the different activities or facets of your personality. Mostly the house depicts your body, but particularly the areas you can associate with your body. For example, the upper floor of your physical house/body is your head or mental attitude. So the upstairs may be associated with your attitudes, the downstairs with sex or reproduction. Because of this a cellar represents your unconscious mind, while the kitchen is about making life palatable or family interaction. The sitting room promotes relaxation and leisure activities; the home office stimulates the intellect or wisdom;

the bedroom is concerned with your intimacy, privacy, sexual life, and rest, or with the state of being awake or asleep to something; the attic deals with your idealism and high-mindedness, or perhaps your desire to get away from people; the toilet your relief from tension or parts of yourself that are unnecessary to you; the bathroom, your attempts to come clean with yourself, or it can be the removal of grime and dirt acquired from your mental or emotional contacts with life and people. The roof depicts protection, security, shelter, or the family atmosphere of love and security under which you find shelter and comfort. The foundations symbolize the basic attitudes and processes upon which your life is built. (see Attic, Basement, Door, Furniture, Glass, Stairs, Window)

HOUSEWORK

This indicates making changes to the way you live and feel. Depending on what you are doing, you may be clearing out old attitudes or things you have held on to, or adding new features to your life and personality.

HURRICANE see Tornado

HURT

This symbol indicates being wounded by what other people have said or done.

ICEBERG

This is usually the same as cold, or ice, namely that you may be holding back, or freezing, your feelings about something. Alternatively, you may have shut down your sensitivity, perhaps to deal with loss, pain or disappointment. Such a huge block of ice may mean that an enormous amount of your energy and creativity is frozen along with your feelings. The iceberg is often used in literature, and sometimes in dreams, as a symbol of consciousness. You are aware of only a small portion of yourself, just as the ice we see above the surface of the ocean is only a fraction of the enormous bulk of the iceberg beneath; much of who you are lies beneath your consciousness. (see Glacier)

ICICLE

This indicates repressed sexuality.

IDIOT

This suggests a lack of reason, or that something you are meeting is not logical. It may mean you are doing something stupid. Sometimes, it represents intuitive knowledge or insight. If this is so you will probably feel the wisdom of the person in the dream.

ILLNESS

Dreaming of illness is often a way of showing you that you have painful feelings that need to be addressed. Often these feelings were experienced, but not fully felt, earlier in your life and now need to be healed or released. At the very least they need understanding. But ask yourself if being ill is the way you get love.

Sometimes dreams about illness show the early signs of breakdown in your body. If you are having worrying dreams, have a check-up with your doctor. Tests have shown that men with serious illness have often dreamed about death, and women with such illnesses have dreamed about breakup and separation.

IMPOTENCE

This is often an expression of anxiety, or excessive use of the sexual function, so it will help to define clearly what triggers the anxious feelings. It can be fear of sexual dysfunction. Impotence can also depict a loss of manhood or womanhood, masculinity or femininity. It may also suggest feeling weak, or being unable to express yourself, or to impress others with feelings or ideas.

INARTICULATE

This indicates a feeling of lacking power or authority when confronted by others, or an inability to express yourself or define ideas. It can be a fear of saying something stupid, of being thought a fool for your opinions, or it can relate to indecision or conflicting ideas, perhaps arising from criticism or punishment during your early years. Working through these problems with visualization techniques when awake can help.

INDIGESTION

This is an accepted idea or attitude that does not agree with you, or it is the inability to stomach something. It may be something that you have taken in, or perhaps something said to you that you did not see at the time was a poisonous remark. Alternatively, the dream may indicate actual indigestion.

INFECTION

This shows the influence of other people's fears, worries, or cynicism upon you, or your own negativity. It may also be a fear of being pregnant.

INFLATE

This suggests to "fill up" or be carried away by a sense of your own cleverness. It may also be superior abilities, knowledge, and power, or trying to achieve a lighter mood.

INJECTION

This is something that is getting into your body or refers to feelings that influence you. This may be wanted or forced on you, or enter you without your awareness. There is often sexual meaning involved, so it can be sex, forced sex, or influences taken in during sexual relationships.

INK

This can be something that has, or can leave, a mark on you, such as a blot on your character. It sometimes represents some unconscious content with which you are dealing.

INSECT

This may imply that something is subconsciously irritating you. Sometimes, it is to do with feeling insignificant. Occasionally, an insect also represents a certain aspect of sex. (*see* Bee, Spider, Wasp)

INTERNET

This is your connection with other people and the world, possibly at an unconscious level until you give it attention. It concerns your amazing possibilities and opportunities.

INVISIBLE

If you are becoming invisible, or appear out of nowhere, it suggests something relating to or emerging from your unconscious, or being forgotten. It can also mean that hidden influences are at work around you.

INVOICE *see* Bill

IRONING

This suggests smoothing out a situation regarding your feelings or attitudes, or trying to get the difficulties or problems out of your feelings or social life.

ISLAND

This can represent something that has come from the depths of your unconscious, but is now established in everyday life—a part of you cut off from others. It can suggest feelings of isolation or loneliness, or your attempt to be isolated from others because of your feelings about them. The island can also suggest the way you feel safe, independent, or trapped.

J K

JACKET *see* Coat

JAIL *see* Prison

JAR *see* Cup

JELLYFISH
This is something that is floating just below the surface of your mind and feelings, yet you feel vaguely uncomfortable or anxious about getting hurt.

JEWELRY
This usually represents love given or received, or the desire to be loved or noticed. It deals with relationships with others, or memories, or feelings connected with the giver, or the circumstances of getting the jewelry. Sometimes, it can be qualities you can develop or have achieved. If the jewelry has a particular history, such as a family heirloom, then it represents what you feel about or what you have gained from your family tradition. Because jewels connect with what you value, they can depict your sexuality. So losing jewels may mean a loss of virginity, or a loss of good feelings about who you are or what you are doing.

JOURNEY
The dream journey is a comment on what is happening in your life, and how you feel about it. It may relate to new experiences or undertakings you embark on. Your life and its events are the journey, and you can travel into spiritual adventures by taking the journey into marriage or parenthood, for example. The dream journey will show you what strengths are helping or hesitations or fears are hindering your travels into the wonderful opportunities of your life.

JUDGE
This denotes your sense of whether you have acted in harmony with yourself, or with the people around you. The judge may be an inner self-criticism that you carry with you and need to re-evaluate.

JUMP
This can indicate you are taking a chance or making a change from one situation to another. Jumping is sometimes linked with the start of flying and can suggest an urge to go beyond your usual limitations.

JUNGLE
This represents the ancient, instinctive urges and processes that are alive in you,

but often hidden. They include the most important directives in life—survival and reproduction. But the jungle of the unconscious also holds the hidden wisdom gathered from millions of years of experience.

KEY

This is the idea or state of mind that allows further realizations or experiences. It is also a symbol of the male sex organ.

KIDNAP

This relates to feelings connected with losing your freedom, or being forced in a direction by others or irrational parts of your own being.

KILL (see Death, Murder)

KING

Dreams often use the image of a king to show a particular relationship with your father—the authority figure or ruling influence. The king can also depict the feelings you have about being ruled or directed by someone, or about your connection with the general influence of your nation.

KISS

This is an expression of love, passion, sympathy, or union. It suggests you are being more sympathetic or understanding.

KITCHEN

This is a place of transformation, where you can change parts of your nature. It

also links with how well you provide for yourself or neglect your body's needs. It may portray you caring for others.

KITTEN

This suggests vulnerability or babyhood, or caring for someone or something vulnerable. It can indicate parental urges, perhaps protectiveness, and may depict a baby, possibly in the womb.

KNEEL

This represents being humble, a receptive condition of mind, or a state of awe. It can also be an acknowledgment of dependence, or even defeat.

KNIFE

This shows aggression, a desire to hurt or wound someone or to use cutting remarks. It can be the male penis. It is also your ability to cut through any existing restrictions or problems. (see Weapons)

KNOCK

This symbol shows something is trying to get your attention, or you are trying to rouse someone. It may also mean that there is a change or something new coming into your life.

KNOT

This represents a problem, or a relationship tangle—a tangle of feelings. In daily life, we may be tied to our work, spouse, or to our mother's apron strings.

L

LABEL

This is a description or "label" you may be applying to yourself. So the contents of the label, or the words it contains, may be about a particular image you have of yourself, or feelings about the quality of something with which you are dealing.

LABORATORY

This may suggest the testing of something, or seeking insight and understanding. It also shows a logical approach that appraises what you are dealing with. Sometimes laboratory dreams indicate mistreatment of your own animal drives and needs.

LABYRINTH see Maze

LADDER

This shows you attempting to get somewhere that is out of reach or difficult to attain. Perhaps it involves risks and anxiety. Depending on your feelings in connection with the ladder, it may show feelings of achievement through effort and daring. The ladder is sometimes a symbol of social success or failure, so if there are such feelings involved, you may be feeling strongly about your social or work standing.

LAMB

This may refer to the childlike, dependent, vulnerable part of you. There are other possible meanings though, such as a new life. This can link with your own child or childhood, and with innocence. (see Animal)

LAMP

This indicates becoming focused or achieving understanding. (see Light)

LAND

If it is undeveloped land, it refers to the opportunities you make to create something from within yourself. This links with your own potential and gives you the opportunity to materialize what is inside you. If the land is developed or farmed, it shows the work you have done on yourself. It symbolizes what you have made of your potential and heritage.

LANGUAGE

This signifies communication and therefore can relate to understanding or misunderstanding. The process of dreaming is partly about verbalizing deeply felt emotions and bringing clarity, so a dream image involving language is halfway toward this. Strange language in dreams is also a move toward clear awareness of what is starting to happen within you.

LANTERN

Unlike the lamp, the lantern usually signifies what shines out from you, perhaps as feelings, understanding, or wisdom. Also, it is the insights or understanding you use to guide you on your life's journey. (*see* Light)

LATE

This suggests that you are feeling that you have left something too late or you have missed out on something. Or perhaps you realize that you have not acted quickly enough to avert a situation or take advantage of it. It can also mean an avoidance of responsibility.

LAUGH

This symbol may be a sense of the ridiculousness of a situation you are experiencing. Laughing in a dream is also a way of dispelling tension and dealing with uncomfortable feelings, or it can even be a prelude to tears.

LAUNDRY

If it is unwashed, it shows the attitudes or feelings that need cleaning up. If it is washed, it displays the changes you have made to your thinking and feeling. Similarly, a laundromat can often be to do with the way you feel transformed or cleansed, perhaps because you have met

a good friend who changes your feelings. (*see* Washing)

LAVA

Powerful and burning emotions, probably arising from real emotional pressure or stress. (*see* Eruption)

LAWYER

This sign may connect with an argument you are having within yourself or with another. It may also be your rational approach to something.

LEADER

If you are the leader, it suggests you feel confident about a certain direction you are currently taking. If you are following a leader, it shows an influence from something, such as an inner feeling that is giving you some direction at present in your life. The leader may therefore represent the confidence you gain from someone, from a special belief, or from whatever is signified by the leader figure.

LEAF

If the leaves are on the ground, they refer to things that were growing in your life and have now fallen away. This can also link with fall (autumn), and the end of a period of experience or growth. If the leaves are on a tree it suggests the part of you that is still growing or absorbing experience. If the leaves suggest spring, there is a link with a new period of growth or change coming. (*see* Fall, Tree, Spring)

LEAK

This suggests energy being lost, or expressing emotion without any control or direction. The energy leak may arise from any number of past traumas, and be using energy to keep them unconscious.

LEFT

If you are right-handed, the left hand nearly always depicts your less dominant or unconscious, or perhaps your supportive, nature. It can also be things outside your awareness. This may be reversed if you are left-handed. There can even be a link with one side of your body, representing the feelings and attitudes you absorbed from your mother, while the other side can represent the feelings absorbed from your father. The play between left and right is sometimes used in dreams to illustrate the dynamic action between opposites in our own nature. (*see* Arms, Legs, Right)

LEFT BEHIND

If you are the one who is left behind, it suggests that you feel rejected or have a sense of not being the same as other people, or perhaps that you want to go your own way. If you leave someone or something behind, it may mean that you are ready for change of some kind. That is, ready to let go of something or someone that may have been important at some time. In some cases, this suggests changes in a relationship if the person left behind is your partner.

LEGS

This symbol indicates the attitudes or qualities that help you maintain confidence and the ability to be independent. Sometimes an event occurs, or you receive news that knocks away your support or self-confidence, and dreams represent this by a problem or injury to your legs. Legs can also depict the ability to get on in life. For example, if your business fails, your ambition may crumble, which can be represented by your legs being kicked away from you. (*see* Left, Limping, Right)

LENGTH/LONG

A long kiss may be seen as a delight, but when length is represented it can also mean boredom. A long working day can indicate tiredness. So look to the content of your dream to see if the length suggests pleasure, importance, or something that is lacking impact in your life.

LENS

This connotes concentration, or focusing your attention or understanding. It may also represent something becoming bigger or more important, or gaining insight.

LEOPARD

Sometimes this represents libido or sexual drives that can appear as threatening. This type of animal also depicts anger or passion. It can also relate to a caring, protecting, or a quick, spiteful response.

LETTER

This shows a realization about something. It is usually about someone else, or news about yourself. It can be a hoped for, or feared, contact with, or expression of, feelings from someone. It can be a symbol used to express intuitive contact with another person. The letter may also depict the arrival of a new event.

LIBRARIAN

This suggests memory or contact with universal energy. It can be the creative or linking process of your mind.

LIBRARY

This denotes acquired wisdom or life experience. Sometimes, the books are very old, suggesting wisdom pre-dating this present life and experience.

LICE

This indicates thoughts or sexual habits that are purely selfish or carry a health risk. It can also be a feeling that other people are like parasites. (*see* Insects)

LIFT *see* Elevator

LIGHT

This depicts your ability to see, understand, or know where you are going and what surrounds and confronts you. This is powerfully illustrated by what happens in the dark, either in

INSTANT INTERPRETER

Musical instruments or music in your dream are a way to become aware of subtle or creative impulses that are emerging. Just as a plant takes shape and color from a tiny seed, so you grow from the formless possibilities within you. Music is the expression of that flow toward life.

dreams or in reality. A noise in the dark can be terrifying because we cannot see its source, but light helps dispel fears and ignorance. This is why when we enter into darkness in a dream it symbolizes exploring the unknown or things we do not yet understand. Similarly, seeing light is the growing of realization, experience, and understanding. Light as a symbol, therefore, represents your consciousness, your awareness of individuality and personal realization. (*see* Dark)

LIGHTHOUSE

There may be a warning in this dream of the dangers of unconscious elements that may wreck your life unless avoided. It can also suggest isolation.

LIGHTNING

This indicates a sudden discharge of tension in a possibly destructive manner. It can be a sudden enlightenment or realization, or a fear of fate or punishment from your conscience. It can also link to revenge or a sudden and disturbing change or release of emotions or sexuality.

LIMP (not firm)
Limp suggests feelings of mild depression, loss of enthusiasm, or even sexual anxiety—the inability to respond to sexual stimuli. This afflicts both men and women and may be due to high expectations of sexual drive.

LIMPING
This is the difficulty, or lack of confidence or strength, you may face in making your way through life. It can represent any impediment in you that makes your approach to life difficult.

LION
This symbol appears in many dreams and usually signifies anger, anxiety, a desire to hurt, aggression, or a fear of these feelings in others or ourselves. We may be afraid of our own anger as it may hurt others in a way that will reflect upon our feelings and desires. The lion can often express repressed feelings of love that can become aggressive if they are not released. The lion and lioness can also represent images of strong parenthood.

LIQUID
This represents the heart, or courage, that can turn to water, meaning that resolves have become soft. Or the heart can melt, suggesting a change of heart, or being open to sympathy. So liquid usually relates to change, to becoming soft, to realize your innate formlessness and flowing nature. Liquid also depicts the movement of feelings in your body. (see Water)

LIST
The list may be a personal reminder of things that need doing, so it may refer to changes you need to make in your life, or things to attend to at work or in a relationship, depending on the setting of the dream. The list may refer to personal qualities, a sort of summary of your abilities or potential. It may remind you of important thoughts, facts, or situations of which you need to be aware. A list in dreams may also present you with choices to make and refer to all the decisions that you are facing.

LITTLE
This relates to something your unconscious does not see as important. It can be feelings relating to childhood or the ability to avoid being noticed. It can suggest feeling small or insignificant.

LIZARD
The lizard usually depicts your most primal and built in responses, such as the fight-or-flight response, the drive to procreate, territorial feelings, or ritual behavior. These are all part of your primitive brain functions and are very necessary. Because of this, the lizard, and

more so the snake, can represent the very process of life in you. This life energy affects your functions and experiences. So emotions, for example, are a particular expression of this life energy. But emotions can be crippling when they are about fear, guilt, and self-incrimination. Therefore, the lizard or snake can also be shown as deadly or poisonous, and needing to be led in another direction. So the meaning is that your emotions and anxieties need some rechanneling. (*see* Reptile)

LOCK

This shows a problem, often of a logical nature, that can be unlocked, if you have the key. It also represents the female sex organs. The lock or locking can depict emotions or tensions we use as a defense, or to stop you feeling something. It depicts an attempt to keep something safe or untouched by others, such as your beliefs or feelings. Locks or a process of locking can also occasionally suggest sexual tension. (*see* Key)

LOOKING

This is being or becoming aware, or indicates your search for something.

LORRY *see* Truck

LOSS/LOST

If you dream of being lost, it links with feelings of confusion, lack of direction, or conflict, of not understanding what is involved in your present situation. The dream environment you are lost in will define your confusion or conflict. Sometimes, this lost feeling arises because there are issues or changes in your life you are not acknowledging. Losing something or someone probably relates to feelings about a lost opportunity, something that you have forgotten but need to remember, or the loss of an important personal quality such as confidence or virginity. People in middle age often dream of losing a husband or wife. It shows them fearing or exploring the possible death of their partner. It is not a prediction, only an awareness of a likely situation.

LUGGAGE

This suggests things, such as habits, attitudes, likes, and dislikes or longings, that you carry about with you, perhaps without realizing. It can also relate to past memories that you are still carrying around, or things that you value. It may also, of course, relate to feelings about getting away, going somewhere, or leaving.

M

MACHINE

This represents things that are automatic, such as habits. It also indicates some form of reason or activity, such as when we say someone is like a machine. A machine may also represent your body's automatic processes, especially something like the heart that keeps pumping. In some dreams people use a huge machine to depict the relentless world activities that can, with apparent carelessness, roll over people claiming their life through illness or other calamity.

MADNESS

This sometimes arises from a fear of what lies beneath the surface of your mind and feelings. It can also represent the torment of a difficult birth, or the search for identity among shattered perceptions of the world and people. Dreaming of madness is sometimes an attempt to deal with, or express, pains and inhibitions that have upset you, and which need healthy expression.

MAGGOT

This represents life or effects in your life that have sprung from parts of yourself that are no longer growing. The effects, however, are usually efforts on the part of

nature to cleanse, heal, or deal with the situation. For example, if there is a great deal of tension in your neck because of pent-up emotions, a dream may portray your neck as full of maggots. Maggots may also appear in a dream where there are fears about death or disease, because maggots often represent the negative view of death as the final decay.

MAGIC

This is your conscious attempt to direct or control your unconscious mind—the eternal force of your being.

MAGNET

This suggests attraction and repulsion. It can be the things you like or dislike.

MAGPIE

This represents the desires caused by material possessiveness.

MAIL *see* Letter

MAKEUP *see* Cosmetics

MALE *see* Boy, Man

MALFORMATION

This suggests that whatever is symbolized is not expressing its true characteristics.

MAN

The man in your dreams is nearly always an aspect of your own feelings, hopes, and fears. Even if it is someone you know well, the dream image is never that person. It is certainly an image you have built from your memories, your views of that person, and also your likes, dislikes, and insights.

If you are a woman dreaming of a man, the man may represent your relationship with a particular man, or men in general. It is therefore about your ability to relate to men. In this sense, the man portrays the power of your own womanhood, indicating whether you can meet male energy with your full female energy. The man can also represent your ability to question social conventions and to attack issues thoughtfully.

In a man's dream the male is an aspect of your own character traits. An old man may depict some aspect of the relationship with your father, or it may be a form of wisdom you have discovered, or feelings about aging. A half-human man shows the fundamental traits that have not been allowed to develop. Childhood training seldom allows these traits to grow gradually into the mature adult, as we are affected by upbringing. So the half-human sometimes comes through in an attempt to grow.

MANSION

A mansion, like a house, shows all the different departments of your life. The bathroom relates to transforming the way you feel, and the library suggests mental growth, etc. The mansion is sometimes used to show just how big you are, how much you hold in yourself, and perhaps the amount of work you have put into becoming who you are. (*see* House)

MAP

This possibly shows feelings of confusion and of indecision about your direction. On the other hand, if the dream is positive, then it can be an indication of what direction you feel is most productive for you.

MARATHON *see* Race

MARK/MARKED

A mark suggests the influence that created the mark. We may be marked by certain experiences of life, or leave a mark through our actions. It may also have arisen by intention or by accident. The mark may represent a sense of ownership or a connection, as with a trademark. The mark may indicate quality or lack of it, for example, a goldsmith's mark.

MARKET

This often shows the everyday situations you face. It may also refer to your contact with the hustle and bustle of the world in general. So it includes the possibility of trade, buying and selling, perhaps of your skills or labor. In some dreams, the marketplace is where you meet a person who represents the highest in yourself.

MARRIAGE

This can be a desire for, or indicate problems in, marriage. What happens at the wedding shows your feelings about or difficulties in facing marriage. It can therefore clarify your difficulties and unconscious attitudes. However, please do remember that dreams often depict your fears; they are seldom predictions. So learn from the dream to sort out your troubles.

Marriage appears in dreams often to represent the uniting of various parts of your being. For example, men often neglect their feeling values and live in their intellect, while for women the opposite can be the case. So, if a woman dreams of marrying a man it may represent the uniting of these two parts.

MASK

This indicates hiding yourself. Or it may reveal a secondary personality, or characteristics that are not predominant in daily life.

MAZE

This often portrays the things and feelings that confuse you. Sometimes you need to admit you are lost and need help. The maze can also depict the difficulties and confusions you face in becoming more mature.

MEAL

This indicates taking in and absorbing life and aspects of the world, and being enriched by them. If you are with others, then it may reflect something about the way you relate socially to people. It could also be a sharing of life and experience with others. (*see* Food)

MEASURING

This may depict how long in time—days and weeks—something will be. It may be saying how "big" something is in your life, or even how you measure up to your own or other people's expectations.

MEAT

To eat meat in your dream is to partake of physical experiences or material values. Meat also represents sexual or sensual experience, physical strength, or prowess.

MECHANIC

This is your means of dealing with habitual reactions to life. Your skill at dealing with problems, such as when you can't get going in the mornings, or on a project.

MEDICINE

This is healing energies that can be released into your conscious life, or positive changes that can be made to happen. Sometimes it means you are being made to, or need to, take something against your will.

MEDITATION

If you dream of meditating, the dream often defines a form of meditation that suits you. As a symbol, it portrays your approach to yourself, a way of dealing with stress, or an attempt to turn away from the external world.

MEDIUM

A medium may represent your intuition, premonitions; or it can relate to the dead.

MEET

This suggests the way you handle meeting other people or a relationship. The actions in the dream will define this. This is also about the way you meet and deal with the many different aspects of your own personality.

MENSTRUATION

This association depends very much on your age and gender. But if you are female, it can suggest emerging sexuality and childbearing, and the feelings you have about this. It may refer to your acceptance of or conflict with this powerful process of life. In a sense it takes over your body as distinct from your personal desires, which calls for some adjustment. The dream may reflect concerns about pregnancy, or perhaps may reveal that you are expecting a baby. Lastly, the dream may show actual physical conditions needing attention. If you are worried about any such dream, check with your doctor.

MERMAID/MERMAN

This suggests love arising from the unconscious, or the unconscious drive toward reproduction, or seduction toward reproduction. In some cases, it can show your love of someone's image, rather than their actual being. A mermaid in particular depicts the inner image of womanhood, still held in, or emerging from, the waters of the unconscious.

MESSAGES/MESSENGER

This is a way your unconscious makes you think about important things, or gives you information. It can also suggest intuitive insight into whatever the message is about.

METRO see Subway

MICROSCOPE

This is being aware of the underlying and unknown parts of your personality. It can possibly be an insight into how your body cells work, the intricate machinations of your mind, or it can be about your hidden feelings or responses—depending upon what it is that you are looking at through the microscope.

MILK

This generally refers to any feelings or needs that are connected with your mother or with mothering. If you are giving it, it means you are giving of yourself emotionally, nourishing someone or an aspect of yourself. (see Drink, Food)

MIRROR

This symbol has a great many levels of meaning. Basically, it is a looking at yourself, for better or worse. The face in the mirror may not match your own. In self-examination you may come across, or see, the worst or best parts of your personality. These are the things you do not usually see about yourself.

MOAT

This suggests a defense used against others.

MONEY

In many dreams, money depicts your power to change things or do things, or it can be having power, even over someone else. It also links with personal potency and sexuality and self-giving, and what you pay for your desires or actions. It may depict what you value most in life, but occasionally connects with struggle or misery—to exist or to pay one's way.

MONKEY

Sometimes a monkey has the face of a man, or talks. In these dreams, tremendous power seems to accompany the monkey. This probably indicates the union of our instincts and intellect, which releases tremendous energies as conflict is removed. The monkey can also represent the flitting of interest from one thing to another, having no real intelligence, or being made to look like a fool. (*see* Ape)

MONSTER

Most monsters illustrate the effects of past traumas. Some such traumas may have arisen from events, such as having your tonsils out when young, being separated from your mother at an early age, or being involved in a war. In general, the monster depicts your personal fear, terror of death, failure, or impotence in the face of outer circumstances or inner urges. It can show attitudes, hates, and fears that have become monstrous and turned against you.

MOON

The most obvious association with the moon is love, romance, the sentimental, balmy experiences of life. It can also suggest youthful love and affection, the welling up of sentiments, and longing for the beloved. This is also linked with the irrational, the deep inner movements and urges within us, the tides of feeling, desire, or madness. It can suggest the pull and attraction of mysterious, dark, impelling desires, of women's strange, sensual, magical, and overpowering attraction, or vice versa. It can be all the unseen influences represented by the moon's effect on the tides. The new or old moon also symbolizes the woman's sexual organs, because of its shape. Because the moon is the companion of the earth and reflects the light of the sun at night, it is also used as the major symbol of intuition.

MORGUE/MORTUARY

This may depict parts of you that have died through being denied or not used. It may also reflect your feelings about death, or people you have known who have died. Or it can reflect parts of your experience you need to release and bury, or perform an autopsy on to understand them properly.

MOTH

This represents those subtle fears that touch us in the dark, or the blind urge to go toward something without any reasonable cause. (*see* Insects)

MOTHER

To dream of your mother usually signifies the feelings or pains you still feel in connection with her. A mother can represent all we want in a caring and loving relationship, or perhaps all we didn't get. Each of us has a fundamental, instinctive drive to bond with a woman at birth. If that bonding does not take place, natural growth cannot, or does not, take place. So the mother may represent this whole difficult issue of survival, and what happened in those early years of trying to become independent of such extraordinary needs.

MOTORBIKE

This is daring, youthful energy and unorthodox behavior. Sometimes, it also associates with sexual daring.

MOTORWAY *see* Freeway

MOUSE

This suggests the activities within you that are not significant, but are irritating or subtly damaging. It indicates being small or insignificant, or it can be something that gnaws away at you. It can represent the sexual organs, a timid attitude, or fear, depending on your reactions when you see a mouse.

MOUTH

Dreaming of the mouth may suggest something to do with pleasure or gratification. It is also your hunger and sexual pleasure. The mouth represents the quality of the things you say, literally what comes out of your mouth in words. Not being able to open your mouth can suggest that you regret having said certain things and need to hold your tongue, or cannot express something. When you are pulling things out of your mouth, it shows you trying to clear yourself of any emotions or attitudes that are not properly expressed. (*see* Chew)

MOVIE

This is sometimes a way of looking at a part of your behavior, or experimenting with feelings, as something outside of you, rather than confronting them as part of yourself. The theme of the film is usually important, because it will illustrate something relevant to your own life. In some cases it is an urge to escape from what is pressing in your life. (*see* Cinema)

Healing dreams

May, a woman who had suffered years of depression due to being alienated from her father and family, dreamed that her son was the size of a small cartoon character. He sprayed her with a magic spray and this made her small, too. Her son led her to her father, who was sitting on a park bench. May said, "I hesitated, feeling I could not go to him. My son told me not to worry. He said, 'If you can't love your father, I will love you both.'" May then saw how silly it all was, and she and her father laughed, and "got the feeling of forgiveness and saw how we had wasted all those years because we didn't have the simple love of a child."

May has now reconciled with most of her family, although, she says, "I doubt if they can understand the reasoning behind it. Although life still has its difficulties, I now have this wonderful feeling of well-being."

Through her dream, May tapped into an experience of forgiveness that was not usually a part of her nature. If it had been, she would not have held a grudge and suffered from depression for so many years.

Your feelings and ideas can often stand in the way of allowing healing to take place. If that were not so, we would all be made whole each time we slept and dreamed. Instead, ideas, grudges, old hurts, or even the beliefs that we hold, can block the healing process. For example, the idea that the healing we seek is far off, or that we must be deserving of it, are blocks. If you imagine you are truly opening yourself to be healed, this will start the flow of healing dreams.

MUD

In some dreams, as in a muddy road or swamp, the mud is simply the retarding aspect of your hesitations and fears. In other dreams, people search through or dig in the mud, which represents the cleansing of emotions caused by outer circumstances, the looking through the experience or muck of your life for its treasure, for often a flower or jewel may be found in the mud. Mud is like clay, which can be molded, so it may indicate the "shaping" of your basic memories and emotions. Mud may also symbolize healing, as it contains all the elements of the past, which we need for completeness.

MUMMY (Egyptian)

This is the attempt to preserve yourself as you are, instead of allowing the constant change, death and rebirth that life always brings. This only results in mummification or desiccation. The mummy may also appear in your dreams when a partner or someone very close to you has died, and there are still difficult feelings about them you need to resolve.

MURDER/MURDERER

This suggests a repression of your feelings or areas of your life. A man may kill his love for a woman because she does not come from a wealthy family. Or we may kill our feelings because we are ashamed or feel guilty about them. We may kill a creative streak in ourselves because of feelings of incapability. The murderer is a representation of a fear that is threatening to, or is, killing our feelings and energy. A trauma can often lead to murderous rage, which is held deep in the unconscious and is only represented in some dreams. (*see* Death)

MUSCLE

This represents physical strength, a sense of being outwardly forceful and impressive. Some muscle dreams actually refer to what is happening in your muscles.

MUSIC

This indicates harmony in yourself, or feelings that are harmonious and emotions that heal and soothe, or stimulate and rouse you.

MUSICAL INSTRUMENT

This symbol shows how well you are able to express your flowing feelings and spontaneous creativity. In some dreams it links with what you feel about sex or your genitals, and how well you can express your pleasure and those feelings. If it appears as a large and complex instrument, it may be depicting your mind.

MUTE

If you cannot speak in a dream, this is an inability to express inner feelings. (*see* Inarticulate)

N

NAIL

This is binding power or the strength to hold together in the same way as a common belief binds people together of opposite temperaments. A nail may also represent, as in Christ being nailed to the cross, the painful links that bind us to our body, our earthly experience, our pains and trials.

NAKED

This suggests revealing your feelings, thoughts, and reactions that you usually conceal. You may disguise dislike with a smile. If you are not pleased to meet someone, you may hide your feelings with courteous behavior, but a child will usually refuse to talk to, shake hands, or associate with someone they dislike. Their real feelings are therefore naked to view. To be naked in a dream may show either a fear of, or a desire for, people knowing your real feelings. It can also be a fear of your real self being disclosed. Some dreams in which you are naked show extreme self-consciousness about other people seeing you. In other cases, the dreamer enjoys being on view, likes people, or the doctor, looking at them. Sexual feelings are often a part of these dreams. (see Clothes)

NAME

Your name summarizes you. So changing your name can suggest a change in the way that you see or express yourself. Someone else's name can depict your feelings and intuitions about them.

NEARNESS

When something is near you in your dream, it shows the strength of your feelings about it, or how aware of it you are. The nearer it is, the more strongly you feel about it.

NECK

You can stick your neck out, which means to take a risk, or have a lot of nerve or audacity. These meanings have arisen possibly from the head being severed in execution, or hanging, or strangulation. The neck is a weak point, and to offer it suggests confidence or fearlessness. So the neck may depict a certain attitude, such as confidence or caution. It is also the point up to which we can be easily immersed in water; beyond that point there is danger. So it can depict what we can take in life, and what is more than enough, which is suggested by the saying, "up to one's neck in it."

Problems with the neck often refer to the way it can act as a bottleneck, or of a traffic jam for deeply felt emotions. In such a case you need to examine what feelings are persisting, what emotions or words you haven't allowed yourself to say. As your neck connects your head (your mental capacity) with your body (your feelings and sexuality), dreaming of it may refer to a split or non-connection between these two main areas of your being that needs to be investigated. (*see* Strangle)

NECKLACE

This is a symbol of power, authority, an augmentation of personality, social attractiveness, or it can denote a charm or an amulet. It may also represent the things you hang round your neck, such as a millstone, obligations, difficulties, or setbacks. It may link to the person who gave it to you and your relationship with them. (*see* Jewelry)

NEEDLE

This indicates sharp pain, self-searching, or the male sex organ. It is the ability to mend things, such as a relationship or situation.

NEIGHBOR

This probably depicts the qualities you feel the neighbor has; neighbors may be helpful or grumpy. Or it may also be used as a male or female symbol. (*see* Man, Female)

NEST

This is the female sex organs or the womb or womb consciousness. It indicates protection, relaxation, warmth, home, or homemaking, parenthood, or a nest egg.

NET

This is the subtle aspects of emotions, words, or a relationship in which you may get trapped. It can be attitudes in yourself or others that may trap or imprison you. It can also be the ideas and beliefs you hold that entangle you in conflicts, and which can restrict your response to life.

NEWS/NEWSPAPER

This symbol is something that is commonly known. It can be thoughts or memories that you are becoming aware of, or already know about. It can also be consciousness as distinct from unconsciousness.

NICKNAME

This probably associates with feelings you have, or memories that are connected to the person or people who gave you the nickname. It can also be whatever you feel about the name. (*see* Name)

NIGHT

There can be many different associations with night in your dream. So try to define what you are feeling. Some possibilities are: not understanding clearly what is going on around you, anxiety about being in the dark, feelings of freedom because you are no longer on view in the light, relaxation and mellow feelings, intimacy and freedom to express yourself. (*see* Black, Dark, Light)

NINE

This relates to the fact that all numbers rise in series of nines and then begin again, and that human babies are born in the ninth month. So seeing the number nine symbolizes the completion of a process, or stage of growth. There are also, in some mythologies and religions, nine orders of angels or forces. (*see* Numbers)

NIPPLE

This represents infantile feelings of longing or hunger, mixed with sexual feelings of pleasure. (*see* Breasts)

NOISE *see* Sound

NOOSE

This connotes feelings about being caught or trapped, or a desire to catch or trap. It can be a fear of, or desire for, death.

NUCLEAR WEAPON *see* Atomic Bomb

NUMBERS

These are difficult to define and are very often only connected with personal associations. They may refer to a particular year of your life, a number of a house you lived in, a date that something happened, how many children you have and their order of birth. They may also draw your attention to these events and emotions surrounding them. Sometimes they may refer simply to multiplicity or size—a crowd of events, a big experience, or a many-faceted realization. However, since humans first counted numbers have had a fascinating, mysterious and even magical significance. In this way, early humans discovered inner qualities in numbers, or possibly unconscious wisdom. Dreams often use numbers in the same way. (*see* One, Two, Three, etc.)

NUT

This shows a fool. It is also the symbol of the inner self, or the kernel of truth.

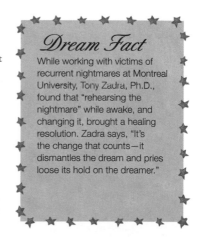

Dream Fact

While working with victims of recurrent nightmares at Montreal University, Tony Zadra, Ph.D., found that "rehearsing the nightmare" while awake, and changing it, brought a healing resolution. Zadra says, "It's the change that counts—it dismantles the dream and pries loose its hold on the dreamer."

O

OAR

This is a means of steering your life through the influences or currents that try to take you off course. It may also have a phallic significance due to its in and out motion.

OASIS

The oasis brings the possibility of being alive and fertile in the middle of aridity and where there is no growth. It may suggest finding or losing a sense of well-being. (*see* Desert)

OBSTACLE

This suggests you are facing some difficulty that you feel is blocking what you want to do, or is opposing or restricting your freedom of action. The barrier can be external or internal, so you need to consider or meditate on what it is in your life that is leading to this obstructive feeling.

OCEAN *see* Sea, Water

OCTOPUS

If you are the octopus, it may symbolize the desire to seize another in your emotions and possess them. Or it may represent fear of being possessed by such emotions, either in you or in another.

One psychiatrist, Hadfield, has pointed out that a baby at its mother's breast often seizes upon her in this way while suckling. So sometimes the octopus represents feelings you have about your mother. The octopus can also represent terrors that drag you down.

OFFER

To offer something in a dream, or be offered something, usually depicts some sort of change, perhaps one in which a decision has to be made about whether you are going to accept or not. It may also suggest extending yourself, or being reached out to in some way. This may involve some level of risk or exposure to rejection or being used.

OFFICER/OFFICIAL

This mostly symbolizes the part of you that is in control of a particular part of your emotions. A love for a husband and children may act as a controlling factor on desires to have a good time with others, or over innate laziness. A fear of being a nobody may direct ambitions and plans. Sometimes, it represents a feeling of confidence or wholeness that brings authority to guide and direct. It also associates with any dealing you have with authority, and what this brings out in you. So it may refer to your father in some way. It can therefore show how you "authorize" or judge your actions.

OGRE
This symbol indicates temper, anger, or a lack of sympathy or understanding that devours or crushes others. Or it can be a symbol of the same thing in others, and how we relate to it. This may be a childhood impression of a parent.

OIL
This indicates how we can pour oil on troubled waters, be an oily or slippery sort of person, or be well oiled. The word is sometimes used to mean flattery, unctuousness, cunning, or working well. It can mean the removal of friction, argument, and disagreement.

OINTMENT
This is a healing or soothing influence or feeling. It can indicate feelings to do with care and contact, or in some cases it may associate with injury or illness.

ONE
This is the first number and cannot be divided. It symbolizes you as an individual, a beginning, or something separate. It is the first manifestation, something that is so basic and fundamental that it cannot be divided. It represents the first cause. You can divide into any number leaving that number unchanged. It therefore represents the power of the unchanging, for example, a hundred divided by one is still a hundred. (see Numbers)

ONION
This may represent crying or tears, or something we find difficult to face. It sometimes represents the layers of your personality. Its symbolism possibly arises from its layers going into a center. Onions have also been used as a symbol to ward off the devil, as with garlic.

OPERA
This sometimes depicts either the dramatization of your inner feelings, the drama of your life, or the stage of life, or the stage of development reached. (see Stage)

OPERATION
This can indicate an inner attitude that may be sick, but which is being sorted out. It may also show a fear of illness, or memories connected with an actual past operation.

ORANGE
This color suggests warmth or wholeness. It shows the influence of the mysterious process of life and life energy. The fruit depicts satisfaction or fruitfulness. Because of its color, orange is often used as a vibrant sun symbol. (see Colors)

ORCHARD
This depicts a sense of possible growth and fruition in your life. It may be that

things have already reached fruition, or that your efforts are leading to growth, depending on the season shown in the dream. (*see* Garden)

ORPHAN

This is the fear of, or feelings about, being unloved. It can be a feeling of being misunderstood, insecure, or homeless, either in mind or body. It particularly links with feelings or fears of abandonment by the person you love.

OSTRICH

This symbol normally relates to sticking your head in the sand because you do not want to see what is happening.

OVARIES

This denotes childbirth and any feelings or fears you have about it. The ovaries also depict fruitfulness or sterility.

OVEN

In common speech the oven is used as a symbol of the womb, for example the phrase "one in the oven" refers to pregnancy. It is also a symbol of the crucible or melting pot, where life changes are made. The oven is a magical instrument because we put in one substance that may be inedible and out comes something quite different. It therefore represents transformation.

OWL

This is about intuition and intuitive wisdom because of the owl's ability

to see in the dark and turn its gaze in any direction. It sometimes represents a fear of the dark or your inner self, or of death or the unconscious—the latter being synonymous. Because of its ease with the dark unconscious, the owl in your dreams can sometimes act as a guide or adviser.

P

PACKING

Packing can connect with leaving home, becoming independent, or being rejected. So analyze your feelings about the last time you packed your bags or house goods as your dream probably looks back to what you were feeling then. It can associate with vacation feelings, and so gives a sense of ease and relaxation. It can also link with making changes or wanting to change. Packing somebody else's bags may therefore mean you want them to go, or you want them to go away with you.

PADDLE *see* Oar

PADLOCK *see* Lock

PAIN *see* Illness

PAINT

There are many sayings that illustrate how paint can be used in dreams. We can paint the town red, paint too rosy a picture, whitewash everything, paint too clear a picture. These sayings suggest releasing pent-up high spirits, being too optimistic, trying to cover up mistakes, or being too honest. Painting can also mean self-expression, showing your inner self, hiding the condition of things with a veneer of paint, or putting a new appearance on things.

PAINTING

This is your works, the things you have done, the picture you have painted of your possibilities and inner world. It is an expression of any subtle realizations or intuitions you have.

PAJAMAS

These represent your intimate feelings. It is the part of you only shared with people to whom you are close. It often indicates a feeling of closeness to someone emotionally or sexually. (*see* Clothes)

PALACE

Your dream palace may be indicating that you are exploring, or beginning to become aware of, the qualities and potential you have inherited from your cultural upbringing and forebears. It may also suggest class roles and privilege.

PAN

If this is a cooking pan, it may link with the care you give to yourself or your family, with everyday life and its needs, or it may represent some sort of receptive situation. A cooking pot is similar to an oven. It can also mean a receptive part of you that receives new things and is open to change. (*see* Cook, Food, Oven)

PANTIES (underwear)

This represents your hidden feelings—your sexual feelings and desires. (*see* Clothes)

PANTS (trousers)

Very frequently these depict your sexual feelings, your desires, or what you may be hiding of yourself. (*see* Clothes)

PAPER

This is possibilities, communication, ideas, or self-expression. If the paper has writing on it, it depicts connections with the past, or with other people's ideas and wants if it is their writing. Otherwise, it shows memories or an awareness of thoughts and sentiments you may have forgotten. Paper can also suggest something valueless. Sometimes the word "paper" refers to a project or essay, so it may link with college or work. Paper may be used as a container, so it can suggest contents, or something you have wrapped up inside you. (*see* Newspaper)

PARACHUTE

This is a skill you use to overcome the fear of falling or failing. It therefore suggests a feeling or a technique to deal with anxieties. (*see* Falling)

PARADISE

This may suggest that you are feeling in harmony with yourself. It can also indicate that you have been practicing some form of meditation, and you have felt the timeless state within yourself. The experience of being in the womb is often felt to be paradise.

PARALYZED/PARALYSIS

This is an expression of how fear paralyzes you. Sometimes we become paralyzed because our unconscious fears come to the surface, or urges that we fear arise. We can also be paralyzed by a sense of guilt, a sense of inadequacy, or ignorance.

Sometimes, while dreaming, a person experiences a profound physical paralysis. This occurs because while you dream your brain switches off the voluntary muscles. If you then become semi-awake and attempt to move, it can feel as if you are paralyzed. The resulting fear causes deeper paralysis. If this happens to you, remember that the cause is a temporary loss of control of the voluntary muscles. When you realize this, you can wake slowly without anxiety.

PARASITE

This symbol represents fears, thoughts, and feelings that diminish well-being. It can appear in dreams as a demon or incubus, and represent our own terrors, fears, thoughts, and desires that are out of harmony with our innate energy. We unconsciously give a shape to such subjective feelings as anxiety to make them more understandable. Often, we do not believe the enormous effect anxiety has on us, especially when we repress it with drugs, such as alcohol or nicotine.

PARCEL/PACKAGE

This is usually a memory, idea, or experience you have not explored or opened to your consciousness. It can be unused talents, ideas not applied, or loving words you have not said. It is also the silent gifts of love and support received from others that you may not have appreciated.

PARK

This represents relaxed feelings, depending upon whether the park is light or in darkness, etc. It is also the way you relate to other people or society. A national park depicts your sense of who you are without social restraints or training—your natural self.

PARKING LOT/PARKED

A car often represents a resource you use to get somewhere in the outer world, and the parking lot suggests leaving behind or accessing this skill or attitude. These are the skills or attitudes necessary to achieve goals in life. So it may indicate a switching of attitudes or roles.

PARROT

This suggests copying what others do or say. (*see* Birds)

PASSAGE

This is a way of making a change, or the restrictions you accept to arrive somewhere. It can be the difficulties you face in growing or changing. The passage, like a tunnel, can sometimes depict what you met in being born. It can also link to the rectum (the back passage) and the vagina (the front passage). (*see* Corridor)

PASSENGER

If you are in a car, it suggests you are following someone else's lead. It can be a dependence on other people's decisions, energy, or drive. Or it can be a mutual direction being taken, for example, in a business venture. (*see* Car)

PASSPORT

This is a symbol of travel, of change, of your integrity or identity. It also relates to feelings of confidence about being accepted, facing authority, or going beyond your usual limitations or boundaries.

PATH

This is your life's direction, the ideas that govern where you are going. If you enjoy caring for others, you may go along the path of healing or medical practice. The path, therefore, shows the direction of your predominant feelings. To lose the way, or go off the path, is to lose contact with or become confused over your best interests, or to miss seeing the direction cues around you. So a well-worn path shows your habitual direction.

PAYING

In nearly all the dreams studied that refer to pay, the action is to pay for something such as a fare or goods. Few of them include being paid. This suggests that pay and paying depict concerns about wanting to, or having to, give something of value, either to get something, or to deal with a situation. The payment can therefore refer to what you have to bring to a situation to make it work or to get positive results. If you are being paid, it shows the results of previous effort, or the reward for who you have been, what you have done, or are doing. (*see* Money)

PEACOCK

This connotes pride, what you show outwardly, an attempt to impress. It is also renewal and vanity.

PEARL

This represents a beautiful personal quality that has developed through trials. Pearls can also represent loss or pain. (*see* Jewelry)

PENDANT *see* Necklace

PENIS

In a man's dream, this represents the sexual urge or the male sense of identity. It is all of the male polarity, including the glandular and emotional disposition.

What is happening to the penis in the dream relates to the male identity. It is therefore often depicting a man's own power of self-expression, his potency in expressing himself, and capability in the world.

The genitals predispose his body toward male sexual characteristics. They bring a certain creative explosiveness to his personality, they create urges toward fatherhood and loving his partner, and desires to help his family if he is emotionally healthy. The positive side of these drives is for him to expect his partner to meet his power with her own dynamism.

Femaleness or maleness must not be confused with personality. The conscious personality is a very flexible and shape-shifting thing. It can be male or female in quality, no matter what the body gender. But in dreams, the female is the receptive, creative aspect of this shape-shifting personality. The penis in a woman's dream, represents a desire for a mate, her relationship with her own male characteristics, such as ambition, work capability, and the ease or difficulty in sexual relationships.

PEOPLE

If there are several people in a dream, it usually depicts the way you relate to other people or the different aspects of yourself. It can also be about your social skills or difficulties.

PERFUME *see* Smell

PET

This can have several associations, but is generally about caring, such as a need to care for or love someone or something. A pet is often a source of unconditional love in our childhood, and so can represent that. Pets are dependent, so the dream can indicate similar feelings, especially by children who know what it is like to feel dependent, and have that need neglected. (*see* Animals)

PETROL *see* Fuel

PHARMACIST *see* Drugstore

PHOTOGRAPH

This is usually about memories and all the feelings connected with the person or situation it depicts. (*see* Camera)

PHYSICIAN *see* Doctor

PIANO

This is an expression of yourself in some way. (*see* Musical Instrument)

PICTURE *see* Painting, Photograph

PIG

This shows someone being low, greedy, or having no refinement. But because of the sow's ability to suckle enormous numbers of piglets, it may also symbolize sustenance of a material sort, or motherhood. Being pigheaded relates to stubbornness. Generally, it represents

sensuality that is lost in material vices. It can sometimes mean the power of material experience.

PILL

This is something you can take in or reject that can influence you in some way. The pill can refer to the contraceptive pill and birth control. The idiom "a bitter pill" illustrates another meaning, that of facing a difficult experience.

PILLOW

This suggests restful, relaxing thoughts and feelings. It indicates the softer parts of you, or it can be someone you want to hug or hit.

PIMPLE

This relates to irritating inner feelings that have come to the surface. It can be worries about how you appear to others, or it is a personality trait that is not healthy.

PIN

This is how you connect to things, such as in the phrase "you can't pin that on me." It can mean good luck or minor hurt, possibly from someone else. It also links to painful sex.

PIPE

Pipes sometimes represent connections, the passage of feelings or influence between people. A large pipe or tube may depict a difficult way out of a situation, or big social connections. Crawling through a pipe suggests feelings or fears of being hemmed in, being trapped in the narrow straits or difficult circumstances. It may also represent birth, either symbolically or as intense emotional memories. A sewage pipe indicates the group unconscious—the negative feelings of society.

PIT

This is a possible difficulty you may fall into if you are not aware. It can show you being trapped in the pit by events or circumstances that have come about because of attitudes and desires. It can also be problems or feelings of being imprisoned and buried by your life.

PLANE *see* Airplane

PLANTS

Depending on the plant, this shows something growing in you, or it is your experience. It can sometimes represent your children and their progress. If the plant is shriveled, it shows a lack of life energy in some area of your life.

PLATE

This refers to having "a lot on one's plate"—having a lot to cope with or get through. A plate with food can depict what is in front of you in life or what you have received or earned. It may also suggest your needs or appetites.

PLAY (in a theater)

This is often a way of bringing a theme to your attention. The theme often refers to something important. The play may also be a way of exploring things, such as a relationship or a dangerous situation. This allows you to practice dealing with it. It can also be the "play" of thoughts or emotions. The play is usually happening in the public eye, so it may include the theme of being seen, being liked, or judged.

PLAYING

This shows a way of experimenting and practicing skills without too much risk. So we can play at flirting, for example, and find out what works in finding a partner. Dream play often has this element of trying out things without commitment, or being creative.

PLUMBING

This is the flow or control of your emotions. A burst water pipe may therefore represent being very emotional. Or it can depict an actual physical ailment, possibly in the intestines or the "water works"—the urinary tract.

POCKET

This indicates your memory, your inner reserves of vitality or money, your capabilities or tools. It is also what you possess or carry through life. It sometimes depicts the vagina.

POISON

This is a warning that you may be taking in something that can harm you mentally, emotionally, or physically.

This may be in the form of words, thoughts, or substances.

POLICE

This is the discipline put on our actions, and therefore our social code, our sense of right and wrong, or how we wish to appear in the eyes of others. The policeman does not necessarily represent your most important directions, but only social or moral codes. These, like the country's laws, can change arbitrarily and be replaced by others. The policeman is, therefore, most often a symbol of how we feel about outer and social relationships. He often links with ideas or feelings about punishment, and behavior influenced by needing to conform to orthodoxy or uniformity. The policewoman is similar to the policeman, but gives more of a feeling of personal connections, sympathies and feeling values than from conscious or unconscious feelings of wrongdoing or guilt.

POOL

This is the inner world of your mind and imagination. It particularly links with looking into yourself and becoming aware of what you are feeling or daydreaming. Sometimes, if you are in the pool or remember being in the pool, it may be referring to a time, perhaps in the womb, when you felt connected with all living things through a shared awareness.

POP STAR see Celebrity

PREGNANCY

If you are physically pregnant, it relates to this state, and the fears, hopes, attitudes, desires, and your physical condition regarding it. It can also depict the development of a new approach to life, a new outlet of expression. If you are pregnant, don't be too worried by anxiety dreams about the baby as virtually all women have them. Only worry if they persist. A doctor can check to see if you are just being anxious or intuitive. Research has shown that frequent anxiety dreams actually reduce tension during delivery.

PREHISTORIC/PRIMEVAL

This represents deep levels of the unconsciousness. It is levels of your being that developed in past ages, but which are being given to you as a physical and mental heritage. We feel these as instincts, or as profoundly strong reactions to situations. It is the part of us that makes the hair stand up at times when we sense something we do not understand.

PRESENT see Gift

PRISON

This is often feeling imprisoned by your inability to cope with circumstances, moods, or relatives. You can feel trapped by inadequacies, fears, or ambitions. It can be any limiting inner or outer influence. You can be imprisoned by an idea or a fear, blaming others for your

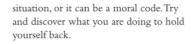

situation, or it can be a moral code. Try and discover what you are doing to hold yourself back.

PRIZE

This suggests a gain in self-understanding or insight through your endeavors. It can be achieving something valuable, or a desire to win, or be superior. It can be a fear of losing or feeling rewarded. It is occasionally intuition about forthcoming acclaim. It can also be that you are seeking praise and recognition.

PUB *see* Bar

PULLING

If you are pulling something, it shows you being active about a problem you are confronting—you are pitting your will against something. If you are being pulled, it suggests an influence that is affecting you in some way. Perhaps you are being pulled by your emotions, or you are attracted to someone.

PUNISHMENT

This may be showing the way you punish yourself or feel pain because of the beliefs you hold or the standards by which you live. Sometimes, it illustrates the struggle between your natural impulses and your social training or conditioning.

PUPPET

This suggests being controlled by another's whims, or being controlling

in the same way. It can also indicate you are being made a puppet of your own desires, by a love of whisky, religious ideas, or betting, for example.

PUPPY

This symbol often depicts all the things we love or hate about babies and children, such as their spontaneous and thoughtless behavior and exuberance. It can also represent a baby, or desire for a baby, or feelings about your childhood. Like a baby, the puppy is deeply dependent and can be neglected. So the starving puppy in your dream shows the neglect of your own lively enthusiasm, or how it was neglected in childhood.

PURSE *see* Bag, Wallet

PUSHING

If you are pushing, it shows your positive action. It may involve opposition in some form, depending on the dream content. But pushing can also mean being in control, or even venting anger. Occasionally, it is about making a stand or holding your ground.

PYJAMAS *see* Pajamas

Q R

QUEEN
These are your feelings connected with your mother. It can also represent your ruling passions, or a desire to rule over others emotionally, or to be respected. It can refer to your need for recognition and acclaim.

QUICKSAND
This relates to feelings of hopelessness that swallow up all plans, hopes, or efforts. It can be a fear of losing ground in competition with others or be about emotions that engulf you.

RABBIT
This suggests vulnerability, sexuality, and sometimes an object of sacrifice or killing. This is because it represents your own vulnerable feelings and hopes that you may have "killed" in some way. The rabbit hole depicts the journey into yourself and what you may discover within. (*see* Animal, Hare)

RACE
This depicts feelings of competitiveness, questions of capability, worthiness, success and failure, or a fear of losing or being inferior. It can also show your passage through life, your participation in the human race, and how you feel you have performed. What you do in the race, how you feel, may show what you put into your life and creativity. If you are in a marathon, it depicts the drama of human life, with all its possibilities. What you do in the marathon shows how you choose to "run" your life.

RADIOACTIVE
This relates to powerful energies arising from within that seem to threaten your conscious self. It can be contamination, or harm through unconscious influences, such as unnoticed emotions picked up or radiated from others, which have influenced you negatively.

RAFT
This is a flimsy philosophy, or half-formed ideas to cope with life. It can be a purposeless relationship. But it can also be a lifesaving change in yourself.

RAILS/RAILWAY
The rails themselves represent orthodoxy, the accepted or habitual way of going about things, or moral values. The train often depicts the train of events that carry us or other people along, or a direction we choose to take along with

others. The engine depicts the energy you put into your activities or direction. The carriages are the events or influences, or things that happen: the train of experiences or events that follow in the wake of your actions. They can also be the compartments of your life.

A train or railway station depicts your efforts or desires to get somewhere, to go on a journey, to find fresh territory, new friendships, opportunities, or understanding. It can suggest travel for new experiences or self-development. Self-analysis is often symbolized as a journey. Leaving someone behind or being left behind suggests feelings about losing someone or being left. The train journey shows your journey in life, since it connects with the direction other people are taking. So it can at times also relate to aging and the stages of life that we all experience.

RAIN

Generally, rain symbolizes emotions or a release of feelings. If the rain is gentle, it is usually a relaxing experience and suggests a release from ideas and intellect. If it is a downpour and storm, it is feelings that may make you withdraw. If the land is flooded, then our common sense is lost to sight in the emotions that are released, and danger may threaten. But rain may also show a return of normal feelings after a long spell of dry intellectualism or a drought of feelings.

RAINBOW

This is an agreement, a harmony between yourself and your whole being.

RAM

This suggests tenacity, strength, toughness, leadership, and power. The sacrifice of the ram is a surrender of this strength to the guidance of your inner self.

RAT

This can refer to underhanded activities carried out without admitting the real motives, such as sex without love or for material gain. A rat is also said to represent time gnawing away at your life, leaving emptiness. It can depict what we most hate or what we feel is repulsive.

RAVEN

This represents death, fear, or the unknown. It is the dark intelligence, the forces in life that seem to have intelligent direction, yet which are not visible. It can be the negative aspect of your father.

RAZOR

This is sharp intelligence. It is the ability to cut through useless or misleading information to get to the real issue. It can depict the thin dividing line between extremes, wisdom and folly, life and death, genius and irrationality, the inner self and the universe.

READING

This is realization, thinking, looking at yourself, reviewing ideas, considering

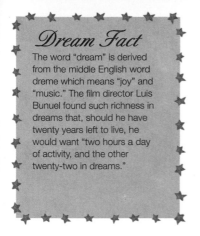

something, memorizing data, or memory. It sometimes shows a way of escaping into fantasy. (*see* Book)

RECEIVING

This is usually about receiving something, such as feelings from a relationship, or ideas that prove to be helpful. (*see* Giving)

RED

In many dreams, this links with experiencing strong feelings, even to the degree of horror. So there are probably some issues to explore when red suddenly appears in your dream. Red also represents your primal emotions, the earthy side of your nature, and your sexuality. It depicts your strength, your vitality, and also your power to heal. Because of its known association with

traffic lights and brake lights on cars, it may sometimes be used as a warning, or a way of saying "stop" or "no."

Because red links to blood and health, being alive, and the process of childbirth in women, the color red often indicates strong and powerful forces that are working within you. On the other hand it can indicate emotional pain. (*see* Colors)

REFLECTION

Reflections from a mirror or water, especially if they show your face or body, usually represent the image you have of yourself or how you feel about yourself. Sometimes what you see is an unconscious image from the past that needs some re-evaluating. Ask yourself where those feelings or that image arose from and then you can reappraise it.

REFRIGERATOR

This suggests cooling off in some respect. It can relate to feeling cold emotionally or sexually. Or it can be a relationship on hold.

RELATIVES *see* Family

RENT

This relates to the amount of confidence you have in your ability to meet the demands of life. What are the events of your life asking of you, and how are you dealing with the basic living process? If you are receiving rent, then the dream is dealing with what you expect or receive from others.

REPTILE

Any reptile in your dreams may depict your basic reactions to that creature, such as like or dislike, attraction or repulsion. But in many cases reptiles, such as snakes or lizards, are used to portray your very basic instinctive responses to life, such as the fear reaction, fight or flight response, the sexual drive toward reproduction, territorial display, and ritualistic social behavior, such as shaking hands or bowing.

The reptile also frequently shows how you are dealing with such enormous flows of emotional or nervous energy. For example, fear is a great protector, but in human life, because we can keep stimulating our response with our imagination or words, it can become overactive, making us ill. You cannot become fully mature until you learn to meet these ancient drives and integrate them into your everyday life. So it is important to develop a working relationship with the snakes, lizards, and frogs in your dreams. (see Alligator, Frog, Snake)

RESCUE

This relates to an intervention or action that has brought about a radical change in you, possibly from real psychological or even physical difficulty. It is worth defining what brought about the change, so you can use it in the future. Rescuing someone else or an animal suggests efforts you are making, or have made, to preserve something important to you.

RESTAURANT

This indicates sociable and relaxed feelings, or being with, or away from, family and friends, depending upon the dream's content. It can also relate to a search for a partner or emotional needs. But as this is a public place, there may be elements dealing with your social interactions. (see Food)

RESTROOM see Toilet

RHINOCEROS

This relates to being dominant or using your influence. This also applies when you want to use someone sexually.

RIDING

If you are riding a horse or an animal, it shows your relationship with your own spontaneous drives such as fears, feelings, or sexuality. Also, it can connote how you relate to your body and its needs and processes, indicating whether you are in harmony with it or driving it too hard. (If you are riding in a car or train, see Car, Railway.)

RIGHT

If you are right-handed, the right foot, arm, leg, eye, ear, all symbolize conscious attributes as opposed to the unconscious. This symbol may also suggest right as opposed to wrong. For those who are right-handed, the right hand is the active, creative, dynamic hand. The left is the passive, supporting, or helping hand. When we knock a nail in, the right hand does the work, while the left holds the nail, and so on. So it suggests that the right side of our body represents our active, conscious, and extroverted aspect. (*see* Left)

RING

This depicts your relationship with the person who gave it to you, perhaps the reason it was given, or the feelings that drove you to buy yourself a ring. It can also represent the state of your marriage or engagement, or, if you bought the ring yourself, how complete you are as a person. (*see* Circle)

RIVER

The river depicts the richness or poverty of your life energy, the flow of feelings and creativity. Air and water continually flow through you, and if that flow dries up you die. Your life processes, expressed as feelings, can carry you along or sweep you away. If you are drowning, you may feel overwhelmed by the torrent of what you feel. The river can be associated with a snake because of the way that it curves. Sometimes, it represents the passage of time. Going against the river's current is to go against your inner flow, or it may be an effort to find the source or to get back to the womb.

Dreams often use crossing a river to mean great changes. If you are trying to cross the water, it means encountering emotions as you change. Seeing someone going across or falling into a river often refers to your feelings about death. A stagnant river shows some restrained feelings or restricted sexuality, or that you are holding your feelings back.

ROAD *see* Highway

ROBOT

This can suggest that what you are doing is automatic or that you are not thinking about it. It can also depict actions or a relationship that is undertaken without emotion, or alternatively something in which you are not getting involved.

ROCK

This suggests solidity, strength, basic foundations, or steadfastness in the face of storms, problems, or emotions. It can represent rigidity or being unmoved in the face of opposition. Inwardly, it signifies faith to help you through turmoil. Mentally, it represents the ability to understand and not be moved. If the rock you see is sculpted in any way, it shows what you have done with your life that will last through time.

ROCKET

This is the energy and drive you direct into activity. It can also suggest male sexuality. In either case, it suggests taking care about where the rocket is directed. (*see* Spaceship)

ROLES

This indicates the various people who appear in your dreams, and the roles they play are usually representative of the many and varied aspects of your own personality, along with the talents and stances you take. It is, therefore, helpful to stand in the role of the characters and describe who you are, and your capabilities as this defines your own possibilities.

ROOF

This symbol represents the attitudes or strategies you use to keep yourself feeling secure. It shows the family atmosphere under which you live. So a hole in the roof will suggest something that has attacked your sense of security. (*see* House)

ROOM

This is an atmosphere or particular situation. Depending on the dream room, it can be a condition or possibility. A big room suggests your opportunity to do things, while finding a new room in your house is the discovery of new talents or possibilities in yourself. (*see* House)

ROOT

This relates to your origins, your basic consciousness, or things that you are tied to by necessity, love, or connections. It can also be your connection with family or heritage from your forebears.

ROPE

This relates to connections you make with others that are binding, or an attempt to bind something or someone. It may also suggest restrictions and limitations.

RUINS

This can point to any aspect of your past. So it can refer to an old relationship now in ruins, or attitudes or a way of life that existed for you in the past. (*see* Castle)

RUNNING

This is trying to escape from an emotion or fear, or it can be rushing toward something. It connects with fitness, if you jog to exercise. In a few dreams it expresses a sort of surrender to the joy of living and existing.

S

SADDLE

This is a symbol of imposing your will on something or someone, or to be imposed on, or saddled with, something. If you are thrown from the saddle, it can indicate feeling out of control or a sudden change.

SAILING

Whatever happens to you in the boat suggests how well or how badly you are meeting the changes, the tides and storms, or calm waters of your life. If there is someone else with you in the boat, it shows how you are dealing with a relationship, or group project.

SAND

This is time, the incessant wearing away of things, the multitudinous aspects of life governed by time. It can be small irritations or abrasiveness, or a difficulty in progressing. (see Desert)

SATAN see Demon, Devil, Evil

SAW

This represents energy to reshape old attitudes, or it can be masturbation. It can also be criticism, a questioning state of mind, or cutting remarks.

SCALES

These indicate balance, justice, fair play, or careful judgments or decisions. Scales on fish may represent your shining thoughts and feelings.

SCARECROW

This suggests having no life, no spirit, feelings, or worth. It can also be an illusion.

SCHOOL

This indicates your feelings about learning. It is the attitudes and strategies you learned at school, such as interrelationships, class structure, competitiveness, authority, group preferences, habits of behavior, or reactions developed during those years. A classroom suggests a connection with study and a relationship with authority. Sometimes, there is a lot of stress connected with self-evaluation and taking exams.

SCIENTIST

This is your analytical mind, or an attempt to measure life, to discover its usefulness, and how to apply it. It may symbolize an intellectual attitude. It can also be your creative curiosity.

SCISSORS

This is your ability to shape things or cut through barriers or connections with others. It sometimes also suggests aggression, a sharp tongue and the ability to hurt or damage others. (*see* Cutting)

SCORPION

This connotes bitterness, or the sting of bitter remarks. It can be your negative emotional energy turned inward to hurt you, or outward to "sting" others.

SEA

This means to be at sea or lost. Life began in the sea, in the depths. The sea represents universal life, the collective unconscious, where all experience is stored, or the infinite cosmic mind. The surface is conscious life, on which the ship, or you, floats, supported and surrounded by uncharted depths. To dive into the sea is to dive into yourself. The seashore is the point where all our elements meet. The sea holds in its depths, or floating somewhere, vast treasures of all the things that humans have ever done. So it can wash them ashore and bring them to our notice.

The sea also relates to birth and death. To come up out of the sea is to be born, to become conscious. To cast yourself upon, or under, the waters is to let go of the world and your individuality, and to connect to your origins and death. (*see* Fish, Mother, Water)

SEAL (on a document)

A seal depicts a trust, a security, a sign of integrity, which we can abuse or use as power.

SEARCH

This often relates to lacking or missing something in your life. Sometimes you have to search for its cause. Ask yourself what it is that you have lost or what you are looking for.

SEASONS *see* Fall, Spring, Summer, Winter

SEAT *see* Chair

SEAWEED

This refers to growth, or ideas that emerge from your unconscious. It may also suggest feelings and influences that you get mixed up in and threatened by, such as when you go swimming and your leg gets caught in the weeds.

SECONDHAND STORE

This relates to the usefulness of useless items, or a searching for your needs or things you want in what is usually seen as worthless. Perhaps it points to the recycling of past experiences or of ideas, skills, or attitudes you have got from other people. (*see* Shop)

SECRET

This is something you know inwardly, but have not yet recognized outwardly. You may know in your heart that someone does not care for you, but because you so badly want them to, you may refuse to recognize this.

SEED

This is stored influence and experience from the past. It is your potential for a new beginning, or new growth. Seeds can also represent the sperm or ovum. (*see* Acorn, Eight, Germs)

SELLING

This possibly relates to the economic value you place on things, or your struggle to survive. It may reflect and comment on business activities or life-changing decisions.

SEMEN

This depicts manhood or potential, life's essence or personality. It is stored power. It can also link with pregnancy or parenthood. (*see* Sperm)

SEVEN

This can refer to yourself at that age, or to the cycles of life—7, 14, 21 years, and so on. It can sometimes indicate your subtle nature. So it can be the influence of your invisible inner rhythms on your physical body, the cosmic keyboard of harmonic vibrations or energies that bring about your existence. (*see* Numbers)

SEX

This relates to sexual dreams that usually express hidden desires, or the appearance of sex can relate to problems in this area.

Sex is symbolized in many dreams, but where it appears directly it shows that the dreamer is more easily able to accept his or her sexual urges and pain. It is therefore important to understand the setting or drama surrounding the sexual element. This will give information about what is happening with your sexual feelings and activities. Our psychological and sexual nature, like our physical side, never stands still in development unless a pain or problem freezes it at a particular level of maturity. Therefore, our sexual dreams, even if our sex life is satisfactory, show us what growth or new challenge is being met.

SHADE/SHADOW

This suggests feelings of being in the shade, or being obscured by somebody else. It may be partner or parents who link with our feelings of being in their shadow. Usually something is standing in our way, in the sense of not enabling us to see the light or gain understanding. A shadow is also a symbol for our unconscious activities that can control our actions, so it can depict inner feelings that are seldom expressed. A shadow can be a sign of coming events—the shadows cast from the future. This is because we often see someone's shadow before we actually see him or her.

SHAMPOO

This depicts the effort to forget or get over something or someone. It can express the effort to deal with longings, ideas, or emotions, or to cleanse sexual feelings. (*see* Hair)

SHARK

This is a trickster or swindler, or it can be a desire to swindle. It is a threat from within, such as a desire to hit or hurt someone that may destroy you or your self-respect. It can be a fear of death, fear of the collective unconscious, or loss of your inner self. It is therefore the power of the unconscious, so it is also its protectiveness.

SHEEP

This is being easily led. It can be a sign of being abused, or of accepting advice and help, conformity, or vulnerability. (*see* Lamb)

SHELL/SHELLFISH

This sometimes represents you or your inner self. Or it can be the shell you crawl into for protection against the world. (*see* Crab)

SHIELD

This is your desire for protection, or to protect.

SHINING

The shining person or thing in your dreams indicates that you have touched a stance, a posture of the soul that enables the glory within you to shine out.

SHIP *see* Boat

SHIPWRECK

This is damage you have experienced to some aspect of your self-image, or even your physical body. It can point to the memories and feelings you are feeling surrounding an old relationship or situation.

SHIRT

This represents your prevailing feelings, emotions, or passions, or it also can be your public image. The color in particular is very important. (*see* Clothes)

SHIVERING

This often reflects great inner excitement or conflict, perhaps even sexual passion that is held back or which is conflictual.

SHOES

These very often link with a role or situation. They can point to the life skills you use to deal with the rough places of life. If you abandon your shoes, it suggests giving up a role or a way of life. Walking without shoes may show that you are finding life hard going at the moment and feeling vulnerable, or that you are feeling free. (*see* Clothes)

SHOOTING

This is a hurt received or given. It can be fears or worries about death, or the destruction of a part of yourself by another that is draining your energy in an aggressive way. It sometimes links with criticism given by someone else.

SHOP/SHOPPING

This suggests exploring the possibilities in life, the decisions that you can make, the variety of attitudes or activities you can choose from, or it can be something that you are searching for or that you really want.

SHRINK

This connects with losing power and presence, or changing relationship to things. It can show a return to childhood feelings or perspective. The shrinking of other things suggests they are becoming less important or less powerful to you.

SICK

If you are vomiting, it indicates the feeling of having thought, felt, or expressed things that do not agree with your emotions. You may be trying to discharge disturbing but usually unconscious feelings or personality traits that you adopted, but which feel foreign to you. (If you are unwell, *see* Illness.)

SIDE

Something on the side connotes something that is not a real pleasure, or real work, not your greatest goal. It is not confronting you, but it may be a support in some way. It is in fact a "side issue."

SIDEWALK

If it is on a specific street, you know it links with your feelings and experiences of that place. In general, it depicts the ease or anxiety you feel about being among other people, or being open to the opportunities and dangers of life. But the sidewalk is also a place of reasonable safety from the dangers of the road, so it is about your skill in traversing the risks of daily life.

SIGNATURE

This is your agreement. It is the mark you leave in the world, or what you want to happen. It is your subliminal influence.

SILVER

When it is silver hair, it suggests age and mellowness, perhaps influences from the past. It often has to do with feelings emerging from deep within, perhaps because of the way it reflects and mirrors things. (*see* Moon)

SINGING

This suggests a sense of harmony with others or yourself. It can be an expression of this inner harmony or your creativity.

SINKING

This is the feeling of losing your control over circumstances or a relationship. It can be a loss of confidence, or possibly feeling overwhelmed by emotions.

SISTER

This sister may represent qualities in yourself, but they depend on how you feel about her, what age she is in relation to you, and whether you are her brother or sister. So she may depict your feeling side, or an under-expressed part of your personality, rivalry, or feelings of kinship.

SIX

This may depict balance, harmony within a group. (*see* Numbers)

SKIN

This is the way you relate to the world through sensations and contact. It can also depict how you handle criticism and difficulties, as in being "thick-skinned" or "thin-skinned."

SKIRT

This is how you are expressing your sexuality or femininity. The style and colors shown are part of the statement. (*see* Clothes)

SKY

This refers to your mind and the unexpected things that can come from it. It also implies moods, depending on whether it is bright or gray. Things in the sky that are threatening or strange depict distressing things on your mind or ones that cause anxiety. The sky is also huge and can show you the immense potential you have.

SLEEP

To dream of being asleep means there is something of which you are not consciously aware.

SMELL

This depends entirely on the odor, and what emotions surround it. A perfume can remind you of a particular person and trigger your feelings about them, or it can evoke particular memories or special feelings or moods. Odors often represent feelings of attraction or repulsion. They can link to fresh or stale food, or be associated with the act of living or dying. They can also represent feelings radiating from you, or from what you sense intuitively about others.

SMOKE/SMOKING

Smoke in a dream may suggest danger, or can be intuition about something. It can relate to passions that are about to burst into flames. (If smoking a cigarette, *see* Cigar/Cigarette.)

SNAIL

This shows how a snail withdraws quickly into its shell, so this symbol sometimes represents a sensitive situation that makes us withdraw from life. It can suggest vulnerability, or hiding in a protective shell of feelings.

SNAKE

This is your innate life energy. It is a symbol of inner wisdom, or knowledge of life's secret processes, and of medical healing. The snake can shed its skin, and so symbolizes self-renewal or rebirth. It can connote attraction and repulsion, sexuality, love, sympathy, emotion, thoughts, higher consciousness, movement, and emotions we create that cause illness. This is the snake's poison. (see Reptile)

SNEEZE

This is a spontaneous cleansing of yourself, caused by the inner healing processes rather than conscious intention.

SNOW

This is usually frozen or repressed feelings or emotions. It can sometimes be purity, or dormancy, such as in winter, when the seeds and roots rest in the earth or unconscious until the arrival of spring. It can also be the ideas, morals, or thoughts that have frozen your feelings.

SOAP

This is an attempt to come clean, to be free of guilt or something that exists in your conscience. It can also be something that makes you feel grubby. (see Washing)

SOCKS

This is generally to do with how well you present yourself socially, but from afar.

SOLDIER

This symbol suggests some sort of conflict. You may be fighting urges within yourself, or struggling with a decision. There can be a drive because of personal growth to face old hurts, but you are shying away from pain and conflict.

SOLICITOR see Lawyer

SON

This connotes feelings or worries concerning a son. It is the growing part of you. It can be hopes or worries about the future, or your extrovert self, desires connected with self-expression, or parental responsibility.

SOUND

If you hear sounds in your dream, it directly relates to what you feel as you dream the sound. Does the sound you hear produce some pleasure, anxiety, or puzzlement? Whatever it is, consider what that means to you in your normal waking life. Also, you can project your will with sound. So the sound may also be carrying a force that is going to make something happen.

SPACE

This is opportunity or potential. It is also the amount of freedom you have, depending on the space. Cosmic space usually concerns the vast potential of your mind and what lies behind it, so it is experience beyond thinking.

SPACESHIP

This either suggests being "spacey," i.e., not down to earth, or the way you move beyond the usual boundaries of your thinking and actions. (*see* Rocket, UFO)

SPEAKING

This is about communication and the exchange of ideas or feelings. While awake, let yourself play with the sounds made in your dream to see if you can get any clarification. Making a speech suggests a desire to make yourself understood to others, to see your inner feelings at work in the world, or to be acknowledged. (If you dream of finding it difficult to speak, *see* Inarticulate.)

SPECTACLES *see* Glasses

SPELL

Having a spell put on you, or casting a spell, can indicate something that has caused a powerful association between an event, a situation, and a person, or it can show strong positive or negative emotions. Such emotions can happen while under anesthetic or when you are deeply involved with someone.

SPERM

This suggests a germ of an idea, or the wonderful potential behind life. It is sometimes used in dreams to suggest energy. It can also be an image of the duality of life and the need to commit to an interdependent relationship to unfold inner qualities.

SPIDER

This refers to any emotion or desire that devours the strength or purpose of your life. The spider is also sometimes seen as a symbol of sexual orgasm, but only if you are terrified, disgusted, or guilty about such feelings. Sometimes, it symbolizes a mother's power, as in the way you are caught in the web of her desires and emotions, and so it can represent an inability to break away from the mother. It can also depict you drawing away from fearful things. (*see* Web)

SPIRIT *see* Ghost

SPORT *see* Games

SPRING

This season's appearance is about a new beginning in some area of your life, or some growth. It is a time of coming alive and renewal. Spring water suggests free flowing feelings and rejuvenating energy. It can refer to your source of life and consciousness, especially if the spring is in a cave or underground. (*see* Water)

STABBING

This either refers to aggressive activities, hurtful words, feeling hurt, or strong sexuality. Sometimes we stab someone else in a dream to break the connection with what they represent, or to kill off unwelcome feelings. (*see* Weapons)

STAG

This represents the masculine, a male, the male aspect of the personality, or male sexuality.

STAGE

This can refer to your life in general, your stage of development, or what drama is being enacted in your feelings. It can also suggest a desire to be in the limelight, or to be the center of attention. The theme being dramatized is often important to understand, as it reflects concerns in your own life. (*see* Acting)

STAIRCASE/STAIRS

As a baby, stairs presented a huge challenge. To deal with them, you had to develop several major abilities, such as steady balance, confidence, and control of fear. Therefore, stairs represent many feelings to do with achievement, failure, climbing and falling. These feelings also connect with work, relationships, your social standing, or sex. Running up stairs may depict an urge to run away from something happening in your everyday life. Skimming down stairs shows confidence and pleasure.

STAR

This is a hope, a wish, or an ambition. It can be an intuition or a subtle sense of the cosmos and your relationship with it, or subtle influences that shape and direct you.

STATION *see* Railway

STATUE

This symbol connotes emotional coldness, and a person who is perhaps not feeling pain or human empathy.

STEALING

This is a feeling that something is being taken from you, or you are taking something, without agreement. Feelings of being unloved may enter into this, as you will feel you are stealing what is not willingly given.

STING

This is something that has hurt you, possibly words or an event.

STONE

This indicates being unfeeling or having a heart of stone. It can show a frigid person instead of a loving one. To throw stones is to give hardness and coldness, to be unsympathetic, or aggressive to other people. (*see* Rock)

STORK

This represents the soul and is a symbol of birth or babyhood, and perhaps parenthood.

STORM

This indicates difficult emotions, stormy events and relationships.

STRANGLE

This is life or energy being cut off by a fear or repression. Emotions can be held in the neck, so it may be feelings about someone living or dead that you are holding back. (*see* Neck)

STREET *see* Road

STRING

This is usually your connections with other people or situations. It can also be your attempts to hold something together, or to form a tie with something or someone.

SUBMARINE

This represents powerful feelings and urges emerging from the unconscious. (*see* Boat)

SUBWAY

This suggests being underground, and usually represents inner or unconscious feelings or tendencies that influence you. This can include childhood feelings or painful memories that are suppressed or hidden, instinctive or intuitive responses, and deep-rooted family or personal attitudes.

SUFFOCATING

This often reflects the way you relate to your environment, either in a relationship or with work or family. It shows feelings you have no room or opportunity to express. Some types of sleep problems, such as apnea, may also cause this dream.

SUIT *see* Clothes

SUITCASE *see* Luggage

SUMMER

This suggests positive feelings, awareness, the middle of your life, and the power of healing and personal warmth.

SUN

This is the symbol of life, energy, and spirit. It represents the whole of your being, or the source of life and consciousness. To sunbathe means to expose yourself to life-giving energies from within. It can mean to release morals, opinions, attitudes, as represented by clothes, and allow your energies natural expression. It is about all energy and health, happiness and success. Or you can have sunburn or sunstroke, symbolizing exposure to something that is painful and harmful.

SURGERY

If you are in an operating room, it connects with concerns about your health or well-being. If you are having surgery, you may be feeling somebody is "getting at you" in some way, or you may be experiencing inner changes. If you are due to have surgery, then the dream is probably expressing anxieties.

SWALLOWING

This is either you taking something in, or if you are swallowing without putting something in your mouth, then you are holding something back—feelings or a healing process.

SWAMP

This suggests any feelings that bog you down, hold you back, retard you, or undermine your confidence and well-being. Or you may be stuck in values or attitudes that are not helping your progress. Sometimes, the swamp represents the relationship existing between mother and child, or sometimes, though not so often, between father and child. The marsh here represents the difficulty felt in breaking away from parental control, the ties of emotional security. It can suggest, therefore, feeling stuck in a situation or relationship. The swamp can show despair or great uncertainty in a relationship.

SWAN

The swan represents the soul, or sometimes the eternal. It may indicate the parts of your inner life that are not understood, or those which are hurt by your environment or others. It can be the loving parts of yourself that are killed or unloved, and which turn into a swan leaving us with a sense of terrible loss. It can therefore be about how when we are deeply hurt emotionally, we actually "leave" the world for a while and shut down.

SWEAT

This indicates the presence of strong emotion: excitement, fear, being deeply moved, or very intense feelings. If you are worried about your body odor in

the dream it suggests that you are ill at ease about how other people feel about you.

SWEEPING

This connotes cleaning up your act in some way, perhaps by changing and getting rid of your negative attitudes.

SWEETS *see* Candy

SWIMMING

The movement of swimming is an ability to cope with your inner feelings and energies. Being unable to swim in a dream means you have not learned the skill of keeping afloat in the depth of your own feelings and mental life. To swim easily is to have true confidence in yourself and a trust in life to support all your different activities and efforts. To be at home in the water, is to feel at ease with your sexual urges, ambitions, desires, and instincts. To be threatened by the waves or water, is to be afraid of yourself, of your own feelings, to doubt your ability or strength to face life and all its experiences. You can feel threatened by your innate desires and energies. (*see* Swimming Pool, Water)

SWIMMING POOL

This may indicate the way your life is connected with other people, as when we say "we are in this together." But it also connects with relaxation and shared social pleasure. Like any pool of water, it can also depict what is going

on under the surface of your mind, in
your unconscious. (*see* Water)

SWING

The act of rocking is a way of calming
down, and is often used by children or
traumatized people. It probably has this
same significance in dreams. It may also
have sexual significance.

SWORD

This may be your ability to discriminate
and search for truth, or protective
instincts or strength of character, with
which you can help and protect others.
Also, like any weapon, it may also depict
an aggressive attitude or male sexuality.
(*see* Weapons)

SYRINGE

This is generally a phallic symbol. But
it may represent energy, emotions, and
ideas, injected into you, such as schooling,
which may be foreign to your real
nature. It can also suggest something
of only temporary effect. (*see* Injection)

Dream Fact

David Watson, a professor of
psychology at the University of
Indiana, says that people who
are creative, imaginative, and
prone to fantasy are more likely
to have vivid dreams and to
remember them. The possible
reason for this is that they allow
more stimuli to arise into
consciousness.

T

TABLE

This is your connection or relationship with others. It can be communal or family relationships. It can be the basic down to earth facts of life—a table is a table.

TABLET *see* Pill

TADPOLE

This indicates sperm or pregnancy. It can also be possible feelings arising from prenatal life. (*see* Frog)

TAIL

This may have a phallic meaning. Or it may connote your past or background, or even backbone, in the sense of strength and purpose. It can also be instinctive urges.

TALKING

A difficulty in speaking, or not speaking, shows the possibility of restrained anger or difficult feelings, anxiety, or lack of confidence, or an absence of real contact or communication (*see* Paralyzed, Mute). Speaking and not being understood links with the feeling of not being listened to or to frustration. No one talking to you makes you feel isolated or judged (*see* Speaking). Most of us talk in our

sleep at some point, and it is simply an expression of the dream activity breaking through into speech. But some dreamers carry on long conversations to which their partners respond. This is probably a release of feelings while dreaming.

TANK

If this is an army tank, it suggests the aggressive defensiveness you may use when in conflict with others. If it is a water tank, it is stored emotions, perhaps restrained emotions. It may also at times represent your bladder, or indicate that you are retaining too much water in your body. It is also occasionally the womb, especially if something is swimming about in the tank.

TAR

This is generally something to do with unconscious feelings or a sticky, difficult situation. To dig into tar is to attempt to get below the surface of your mind to find the hidden sources of your behavior and feelings.

TARGET

This represents ambitions, hopes, your aims, even your goal in personal growth. Sometimes it is the vagina.

TATTOO

This is an experience that has left an indelible memory or mark. Being bitten by a dog may leave a permanent fear of dogs. Being hurt emotionally by someone may leave a similar effect. A tattoo can also represent how your personal habits or efforts affect you. It may occasionally refer to how you gain identity, or to which group you identify.

TAXI

This is paying for your needs. Or it can be becoming involved with a stranger or someone else to get to where you want to go. The taxi can sometimes represent protection from the sort of threats you feel in everyday life, especially for women. (*see* Car)

TEACHER

This is something you are learning or have learned. It can be feelings developed in school that are still active. Perhaps you are dealing with how you related to authority at school.

TEDDY BEAR

This is a childish way of expressing a need for security or comfort. Like any toy, it can represent the way an outer object can help to create your own feelings of security or companionship. (*see* Doll, Toy)

TEENAGER

In general, the teenager relates to that period of life and the feelings you felt or experienced while you were an adolescent. The teenage dream can be about uncertainty or inexperience in relationships, along with powerful sexual/romantic attraction or feelings, and maturing sexually. Dreams containing a teenager may also deal with concerns about sexual issues, a lack of confidence and experience, and the experimentation of that time. The action and drama of the dream will define which of these is represented.

A dead teenager suggests hurt feelings of love or wanting to be loved, damaged self-esteem, or feelings of value in the world. This often relates to a difficult time in your teens when you killed some facet of your personality or love.

TEETH

Teeth can represent your bite, your effectiveness, or your power in life. They may represent biting remarks or hurtful words. They are your ability to "chew" over a problem, or to get a taste of, or try to experience, what you are considering. If you dream of your teeth falling out, the cause may be a sense of losing someone you love or who is close. This leaves a gap in your life such as you feel when a tooth comes out. Missing teeth also suggest getting older, or feelings or fears about aging.

TELEPHONE

This can be communication or contact with yourself or others. If you do not answer, it may suggest you are unwilling to listen to your inner feelings or intuitive advice, or be in relationships with others. If there is no one on the other end, it suggests feeling alone and perhaps unwanted. An emergency call is probably a desperate attempt to be heard, or a cry for emotional help in a difficult situation.

TELESCOPE

This suggests trying to understand something more clearly, or getting a closer look at things that were not clear before. It may also show you making something big out of a small experience.

TELEVISION

This suggests what you feel, understand, or intuitively know about what is going on in other people's lives or the world. It is being aware of the drama that is taking place in your own life that you may have overlooked. It is also the strategy you use to blank out the world and relax.

TEMPTATION

This is the conflict between different aspects of yourself, perhaps sexual urges and social fears, or personal boundaries.

TEN

This may depict teamwork, or being part of a group action. This also represents a new beginning on a higher level. It is a fresh start, almost as if from scratch, but all the past experience contributes to this new phase. (*see* Numbers)

TENT

This is letting go of civilized aids or ways of life, so it is getting away from your usual situation. It can also signify holidays or youthful exploration.

TERROR

This is an inability to face or cope with the emotions, fears, ideas, or urges represented in the dream. It is important to find out where you felt that sort of terror in the past as this releases its hold on you. This is not easy, because many memories have never been verbalized, or occurred either before you spoke or when you were under anesthetic. But they can be brought to the surface through steady dream exploration.

TEST/TESTING

This is an attempt to deal with the difficult questions or problems that life poses. It is a fear of inadequacy or of being tested. It is about comparing yourself with others, or with the opinion of others. It can be about doubts concerning your fitness and capability in life, marriage, or parenthood, or stress in connection with a competitive job or situation. It may be responses still active from school experiences. Testing equipment may indicate an aspect of your body, or perhaps a skill you have. It may also refer to your sexual capability. Medical tests normally relate to concerns about your health, or can suggest getting pleasure from being examined. (*see* Exams)

Life is an expression of energy. In dreams anything that moves or flows, such as flames or water, shows how you are expressing your energy. Your dreams show if you are blocking yourself, going with the flow, directing your energy, or fearing it. You may even be creating something that is beyond yourself.

TESTICLES

These relate to the power of masculine sexuality and the drive or aggression that it arouses.

THEATER *see* Stage

THERMOMETER

This is a gauge of your emotional warmth or coldness, or it can also be a measure of your health, or it may be anxiety about it. (*see* Cold, Heat)

THIRST *see* Drink

THORN

This relates to painful experiences, from which it is difficult to move on.

THREAD

This is a line of thought or action, delicate or fine connections, or directions that can be easily lost or broken unless care is taken. Or it can mean a fine or tiny idea or energy you

easily lose, in the same way as when life hangs by a thread. It may link with the word threadbare.

THREE

This frequently represents the family: mother, father, and child. But it can be any unity of the positive and negative to create a new condition. (*see* Numbers)

THRIFT STORE *see* Secondhand Store

THROAT

This is an ability to speak or express your own needs and opinions. It is also a vulnerable area. (*see* Neck)

THUNDER *see* Storm

TICKET

To get the ticket is to get the idea, method, or capability. A ticket represents the ability to pass through barriers or difficulties in life, as the price has been paid in experience or self-giving. It can also mean a sense of validity and ease, or possibly a lack of it.

TIDAL WAVE

This relates to a great release of energy or emotions. This may be felt as a great threat, but is simply energy and can be directed. It just needs experience to ride such high energy.

TIDE

This is opportunity or power of events. It is the ebb and flow of enthusiasm,

desires, cravings, ambition, or energy.
(*see* Moon, Sea)

TIE/TYING

This is creating bonds, either in the form of unifying, binding, or restricting. It is also trying to mend something or keep things together. (*see* String)

TIGER

This is power, anger, sexual power, inner anxiety, or terrifying urges. It can be a fear of another person's anger or forcefulness. Sometimes, it is the power of a mother's protectiveness, or it can be a woman's anger or sexual craving.

TOAD

This suggests uncomfortable feelings. It is also the deeply biological processes of your body, of reproduction and transformation, the tadpole to toad process from conception to birth. (*see* Frog, Tadpole)

TOILET

Many people find their only privacy in the toilet, so it can depict your need for, or feelings about, privacy. The toilet is also where you release tension or get rid of things your body no longer needs. So it can indicate letting go of old feelings. (*see* Feces, Urine)

TONGUE

This is your inner feelings, your ability to communicate, or an expression of anger or dislike. It can suggest the male sex organ.

TOOLS

This is self-expression, your capabilities, practicality, and skills. It is the attitudes that enable you to make changes in your life, and your skill to do so.

TORNADO

This is threatening influences pushing you toward things of which you may be afraid. It is pressure in some form. It can be a tremendous mental or emotional energy release that feels as if it may overwhelm you. (*see* Air, Wind)

TORTOISE

This indicates the outer hardness or shell, in which we may hide when others try to contact us deeply. The animal symbolizes slow but patient efforts, sensitivity and shyness.

TORTURE

Torture, in the same way as crucifixion, can indicate that you are arriving at a new freedom or inspiring future. (*see* Hell)

TOUCH

This indicates the degree of relationship with another person or an aspect of you. It is the connection with an influence, and the experience of something other than you.

TOWER

This is either your attitudes that keep you separate and aloof from people, a means of protecting yourself from human contact or conflict, or it is a way of standing above events and getting a wider view of them.

TOWN *see* City

TOY

This is childhood habits, desires, or attitudes that you have not yet outgrown or changed. You may want the sort of non-threatening relationship you had with your parents, or just be seeking love and affection. When we are children, our toys can be extremely important. So a cuddly or soft toy may mean to us the only non-threatening relationship we have, and so depicts security, love, and the ability to control instead of be controlled. It can therefore represent the ability to create, with the aid of an external object, an internal source of love and assurance. As an adult it may suggest a desire for a non-threatening emotional relationship. It can also be a means of venting anger or pain. (*see* Doll, Teddy Bear)

TRAIN *see* Railway

TRANSPARENT

This is being able to see what is going on inside yourself, in other people, or in a situation. (*see* Glass)

TRAP

We are all trapped in old ideas or habits that may have been applicable at one time, but which are now detrimental, such as hurts and responses that still

linger. These traps are often depicted by prisons, snares, barriers, ropes, threatening people, or animals. Finding your way through them is the great adventure of life. Out of this arises your inner strength, allowing you to wake up to whom you really are, letting you emerge into your real life and identity.

TRASH *see* Garbage

TRAVEL

This is your movement through life, your aging process, your search for meaning and new experiences. It can also suggest a way of keeping away from extended, lasting, and therefore confrontational relationships.

TREADMILL

This can be a feeling that life is nothing but work and effort. It can also suggest that you are trapped by duty and the regular demands made on you.

TREE

The tree is one of the great dream symbols, representing your whole physical, psychological, and social growth as a person. The roots depict your connection with the earth through food, air, and water, as well as your psychological roots in family and culture. The trunk shows your body and what you have developed in your life: the main thrust of your expression. The branches are the different avenues you have explored and developed: your children, your relationships and ideas. The seeds or flowers are your own fruition: the expression of what is deeply your own unique creativity. They are also your reproduction as a parent with children or ideas in the lives of others. Dead wood represents parts of you that no longer carry life and energy, perhaps ideas or opinions you no longer hold. A tree that is struck with lightning represents sudden change, even death. (*see* Cross, Wood)

TRESPASSING

This can be forcing your attentions on someone, or vice versa. It can be doing something that you know is invasive or disliked.

TROUSERS *see* Pants

TRUCK

In the same way as a car, this symbol is your means of getting about in life—that is, a vehicle of expression such as music, drives, longings, or ambitions, but the truck connects more with commercial associations or projects. So it may link with feelings of major change, commercial ventures, or moving.

TRUNK *see* Car, Chest, Tree

TSUNAMI *see* Tidal Wave

TUNNEL

If the tunnel is dark, it usually signifies entering into experiences you do not understand and are not fully aware of. It is usually past experiences that are felt but not verbalized or made conscious yet. It can also be entering into your unconscious. It can also be reliving the experience of birth.

TV *see* Television

TWELVE

This number represents completion. For example, the twelve months of the year encompass the four seasons. It also can depict the twelve traditional aspects of human personality shown by the signs of the Zodiac. For some people it can also represent teamwork. (*see* Numbers)

TWO

This usually refers to a partnership, either in a sexual relationship, or as a parent or child, or in business. It also connects with conflict or opposites, or any sort of duality. (*see* Numbers)

UV

UFO

Dreaming about an Unidentified Flying Object (UFO) is probably a meeting with the complete "you," or an awareness of parts of your mind that are usually unknown to you and therefore alien. This new experience, or new way of knowing yourself, is emerging. So the UFO experience often happens before life changes, so you first need to reflect or meditate on what type of changes are occurring inside you. (*see* Spaceship)

UNDER/UNDERNEATH

This can imply a wide range of meanings, depending on the context. When you are under a roof or a tree, it can suggest protection. It can imply being ruled or dominated by someone, or feeling they are superior, if you are in some way underneath them. It can point to your own superior feelings if something or someone is underneath you in some way.

UNDERGROUND (transport)

see Subway

UNDRESS

This is revealing your true feelings. It is about casting off restraining or inhibiting attitudes, fears, or morals. It can be a desire to display or express yourself more openly. (*see* Naked)

UNEARTH

This is about discovering things you have forgotten or not been aware of previously. This can be your feelings about a past love or unconscious thoughts. (*see* Digging)

UNIFORM

This is about conformity and orthodoxy. It is also authority, power, and an expression of a universal activity. The uniform may also depict your identification with a social role, such as that of a nurse or teacher. In this case it may be about how much you need that role for your own sense of confidence, or maybe how you are changing in the role.

UP/UPWARD

In many dreams this points directly to the strategies you use to deal with emotions or situations that undermine confidence or positive feelings. For example, you may divert your attention from something that depresses you by switching the television on, visiting a friend, drinking alcohol, or smoking.

Wherever possible, it is worth meeting the feelings you are trying to escape from in the dream. Do this by imagining yourself in the dream again and turning to face whatever it is you are escaping. Notice how you react, and what feelings or memories arise. (*see* Ascent)

URINE

To urinate is to release tensions, whether they are sexual, emotional, professional, or educational. Urine can also symbolize sexual feelings, or experiences in the womb.

UTERUS

This usually links directly with the ability to bear a child. This indicates childbirth, pregnancy, female receptiveness and the ability to nurture life. While returning to the uterus/womb can represent an infantile event, it really symbolizes the experience at that time. This is a state of mind that is merged with all consciousness, yet undefined, lacking self-awareness. It is also to give birth in some way, either to a child or to a creative project. (*see* Vagina)

VACATION

This refers to being relaxed, or to experiencing a change in your feelings. It can also suggest a change from your usual way of life. It can be an opportunity to express yourself differently, or to meet some new experiences, or it can be an attempt to be happy.

VAGINA

This represents not only sexual feelings and desires, but is a symbol of complete womanhood and femininity. The shape of the vagina represents the human qualities of sympathy, receptivity, loving acceptance, or a desire to absorb.

VALLEY

This suggests a descent into material values, gloominess, outer activity, practical issues, and sometimes into problems and fears. The valley can also mean everyday life with all its variety and richness.

VAMPIRE

This refers to an idea or fear that is draining energy, ambition, or resolution. It can also be a negative relationship that makes you feel it is draining your energy or sense of well-being. It can be difficult feelings about sex or a sexual relationship, or feelings about not being independent, indicating that you feel psychologically linked to someone, such as a parent.

VASE *see* Cup

VAULT

This may represent memories or influences from your past. It can also be something valuable or deeply important, which you have locked away or buried. If the vault is connected with burial, then it depicts feelings you have about death or the dead.

VERTIGO

This imagery suggests anxieties or a loss of confidence. It may also indicate that you are on the verge of something that you usually do not allow yourself to experience. So you sense a vastness that makes you feel very uncomfortable or anxious.

VICTIM

This suggests that you have a passive relationship with others and are not acknowledging or expressing your own wants or needs. It may also be that you are victimizing someone else who is not strong enough to stand against your desires or will. You may be using past hurts to remain passive and to bemoan your fate. This is a form of blaming that puts the responsibility onto other people.

VOLCANO *see* Eruption

VOMIT *see* Sick

VULTURE

This is about feelings to do with waiting for someone to die, or a situation of living off the unfortunate experiences of others.

WXYZ

WAITER/WAITRESS

This may mean that you feel you are providing for others' needs. In which case ask yourself if your own needs are being met. If you are being waited on, it may deal with feelings about being supported or helped, or feeling that your needs are satisfied. This can also be word play for waiting for something or someone.

WALK

This usually depicts personal effort, or making your own way at your own pace. The conditions or surroundings where you are walking suggest what you feel about your progress and your personal situation. The direction in which you are walking shows the aim of your activities and hopes. The future is represented by where you are going. If you are walking backward, it suggests a wrong attitude.

WALLET

This suggests your abilities to deal with external events easily. It can be about confidence and sometimes a sense of identity or value. So loss of a wallet indicates feelings of being less capable or powerful. (*see* Money)

WANT/WANTING

Whenever the words "want" or "wanting" appear in your dreams, it suggests urges or desires you may not be acknowledging well in your conscious life. Sometimes, the urge may be misdirected, such as loving someone who cannot love you in return. But the urge is still there to be loved, and some other source of love needs to be found. When it is a "don't want" in the dream, change it to a positive: "I didn't want to go with my mother" can become "I wanted to do my own thing." This gives an open channel for expression, rather than suppression.

WAR *see* Battle

WARDROBE *see* Closet

WAREHOUSE

This suggests memories or aspects of yourself put into storage, such as potential or ambition while you are bringing up children.

WARMTH

This is physical well-being and perhaps rejuvenation and relaxation. It is also affection and closeness in a relationship. (*see* Heat)

WARP/WARPED

This represents your inner feelings or energies that are misdirected by outer beliefs or fears. It shows getting the wrong idea or it can also be a misunderstanding.

WASHING

This is clearing out feelings such as despair or self-doubt, or it can be fears about health, or possibly your neurotic phobias. Sometimes, this is shown as a healing of past hurts or tensions, even a warming of cold emotions. Washing your hair shows you changing your attitude or the way you present yourself to others, or altering your viewpoint or the way you think about something. Washing the vagina or penis is the clearing out of negative sexual feelings or dealing with the results of pent-up sexuality. Washing your hands shows you getting rid of feelings about something that you have done or in which you were involved. (*see* Soap, Water)

WASP

This is irritability, hate, spitefulness, anger, or vengeance. It can be painful or hurtful remarks or emotions.

WATER

This usually denotes your flowing feelings or ability to respond to people. It can therefore be your emotions, desires, or moods, depending on how the water appears in your dream. If it is muddy, it means your feelings are influenced by outer circumstances, worries, material problems, or values. If it is clear and sparkling, it symbolizes faith, fearlessness, pure feelings, hope, and joy.

Water takes the form of any vessel that contains it. So it represents your ability to be influenced either by fears, hope, understanding or ignorance, love or duty, and so on. This is important as it means your anxieties direct the torrent or energy called emotion. As emotions can heal or kill this is something that needs attention. (*see* River, Sea)

WEAPONS

This suggests fears or desires connected with hurting or being hurt. The weapon often hides a deeply felt childhood pain or fear that has not been dealt with, so it may come out as anger or rage. Some weapons, such as guns or knives, can also represent male sexuality or any fears you may have about it.

WEATHER *see* Rain, Snow, Storm, Sun

WEB

This is something you may inadvertently get caught up in and find it difficult to extricate yourself from. It may suggest a sticky end to a relationship or project. The dream web can also depict the intricate and powerful connections we have with other people and with life. (*see* Spider, Maze)

Shadowy and unrecognized figures often appear in dreams. Sometimes they denote parts of your nature that you avoid or repress—or, at the least, fail to express. In other dreams they help to define attitudes that can transform you.

WELL

This is drawing on your own inner depths and the resources that lie behind your personal self. This may include deeply perceptive intuition or healing. It can also refer to the vagina. (*see* Water)

WEREWOLF

This is your own, or somebody else's, rapacious desires, animal lusts, urges, or hates. (*see* Vampire)

WHALE

This represents the enormous forces existing in the unconscious that are intelligent and upon which our life depends. It is the power to dive under the surface of the mind to become aware of this world that is normally hidden from view. (*see* Fish)

WHEEL

This indicates changes or luck, as with the wheel of fortune. It also symbolizes the ability to get things moving or rolling. (*see* Circle)

WHIP

This suggests domination by someone or it can also be the desire to hurt people or be hurt. Depending on the context, it may also link with sexuality that contains guilt or pain.

WHITE

This can depict feeling cleansed, or awareness, or, if it is used with clothes or a wedding dress, purity. But in some dreams, it links with threat and fear that can arise from many official buildings, such as hospitals, that use the color white. A white animal suggests wisdom and intuitive understanding.

WIG

This represents disguising your real image. It can be worries about your appearance or a need to remain unidentified. (*see* Hair)

WIND

This suggests changeability, the ever shifting mental processes or unseen influences in your life. It can be ideas or other influences that move or pressure you. (*see* Air)

WINDOW

This is your outlook on life, your awareness of other people and outer events. (*see* Glass)

WINE

This is vitality. It is an influence that changes the way you feel, or it can be an artificial means of coping with stress. It can be the social methods used for a person to become part of the group. (*see* Alcohol)

WINTER

This is the end of a season of growth or activity. It indicates rest, inner processes that have not shown themselves in consciousness, or death or inactivity. It is the falling away of outer movements to concentrate on inner consciousness. It can also depict a hard time in life or business, perhaps a period of cold, in the sense of nothing growing in your life, or little feelings. (*see* Cold, Ice)

WOLF

This symbol usually represents fears about your own urges or anger, or just plain childhood fear. Fear is a natural or instinctive reaction, and one of the ways we may deal with it is anger, or by withdrawing, or calling on our fight-or-flight reaction. If you face your wolf, you may gain the power it has and redirect all its emotional energy to you. But the wolf can suggest existing alone, as with the lone wolf. It also indicates an image of caring parenthood and love.

WOMAN

If you are a woman, the dream woman usually depicts some facet of your personality or potential. To define this, use the technique of standing in the role of the dream character. If you are a man, the woman generally illustrates an aspect of how you feel about and relate to women. She will also illustrate the less expressed part of you. (*see* Girl, Female)

WOMB *see* Uterus

WOOD

In general, wood represents ideas, opinions, or habits that are a fixed part of your nature. An old, dying tree trunk represents parts of you that are no longer capable of adapting to incoming ideas and experiences. Cutting up wood, and building new things with it, is to use old ideas in new ways.

However, a wood, or collection of trees, has quite a different significance. It represents not only what has grown in your life and is established, but also what is natural and unconscious. So the wood can represent relaxation, or an inner journey. (*see* Tree)

WORK

This nearly always connects with your work activities, ambitions, or actual work environment and situation. If you are actually working it shows your attempts to change a situation or create something.

WORLD

Sometimes this depicts the "world" or viewpoints that you have created out of your attitudes and responses to events and people, so it is dealing with your personal interactions with them. Dreaming of other worlds suggests different ways of approaching life. (*see* End of the World)

WORM

This relates to being low, possible decay, or earthiness.

WRITING

This refers to expressing your inner self. It can mean clarifying feelings, materializing or recording them so that you make your inner feelings more defined or less vague. It can also be about how you communicate.

X-RAYS

These are invisible influences in your life. It can be a penetrating insight, or a fear of being seen through, or looking at your inner self. It can also be a fear of developing an illness or inner faults.

XYLOPHONE

This suggests something playing on your feelings or sympathies.

YACHT *see* Boat

YELLOW

This is sometimes linked with cowardice, but also, since it is a warm color, with hopeful feelings. (*see* Colors)

ZERO

This is perhaps feelings or sensations of loss. It can also connote the emptiness

we often fear, but it is also the balm of sleep and the quietness that underlies all the noises of physical life. (*see* Numbers)

ZIPPER

This may link with your general appearance. For example, you may be saying, "Is my zipper fastened?" Sometimes it can relate to connections with others or secrecy, such as in the expression: "Keep it zipped!"

RESOURCES AND
FURTHER READING

WEBSITES

www.dreamhawk.com
Further dream interpretations can be found on Tony Crisp's website, Dreamhawk.

www.sleeps.com

www.susanhendricks.com

BOOKS

DREAM ANALYSIS

Corriere, R., Karle, W., Woldenberg, L, and Hart, J., *Dreaming and Waking* (Culver City: Peace Press, 1980)

Delaney, G., *Sexual Dreams* (New York: Ballantine Books, 1994)

Jung, C. G., *Man and His Symbols* (London: Picador, 1978)

Stevens, W. O., *The Mystery of Dreams* (London: Allen & Unwin, 1950)

Sugrue, T., *There is a River: The Story of Edgar Cayce* (Virginia: ARE Press, 2003)

Van de Castle, R. L., *Our Dreaming Mind* (New York: Ballantine Books, 1995)

THE COLLECTIVE UNCONSCIOUS

Bucke, R. M., *Cosmic Consciousness: A Study in the Evolution of the Human Mind* (Bedford, MA: Applewood Press, 2001)

Capra, F., *The Tao of Physics* (London: Flamingo, 1992)

Segal, S., *Collision with the Infinite* (Moreton-on-Marsh: Windrush Press, 1996)

Watson, L., *Supernature: A Natural History of the Supernatural* (Manchester: Coronet, 1974)

Zukav, G., *The Dancing Wu Li Masters* (New York: Perennial, 2001)